Feng
Shui

Feng
Shui

**GEDDES &
GROSSET**

This edition published 2001 by Geddes & Grosset,
David Dale House, New Lanark ML11 9DJ Scotland

© 2001 Geddes & Grosset

Original text first published 1999
Reprinted 1999 (twice), 2000
New edition, text expanded, 2001 by April Simmons
Reprinted 2001

Cover photographs courtesy of PhotoDisc, Inc.

ISBN 1 84205 029 X

Printed and bound in the UK

Contents

Introduction

What is Feng Shui?

Feng Shui is the ancient Chinese art of understanding and organising our environment to enable us to live in greater harmony with nature. The characters which translate into the words Feng Shui are pronounced *fung shoy* or even *foong showay* (but with a short o), and mean literally 'wind' and 'water'. There is some debate about what the 'feng' and the 'shui' *really* represent, however. Some see wind and water as the strongest forces of nature – the 'feng' can be likened to a stream of energy passing overhead just like wind, and the 'shui' is water on the surface of the earth. Thus the term aptly indicates the awesome power of a system capable of governing every aspect of life. Others say the item represents the nature of Feng Shui as 'that which cannot be touched', an intangible force working imperceptibly around us. There is no reason why the two theories cannot co-exist.

Feng Shui effectively manipulates the energies or chi to help achieve a balance between man and his environment. There are many aspects of Feng Shui which are beyond the immediate scope of the individual, such as its application to the layout of a city. However, much of it can be applied practically, and to great effect, in the home, office and garden.

The history of Feng Shui

Feng Shui was certainly practised in China 3,000 years ago but may go back 5,000 years or more. In China it was almost enshrined officially as the science of the state. Hum Yue was the ancient term for Feng Shui – Hum meaning, basically, heavenly path and Yue the earthly path, both referring to the energies of chi. The principles of the subject and the way it is practised are contained in some ancient texts such as *The Book of Songs (Shih Ching)* which was written over many years commencing in the ninth century BC. Significant development occurred in the Han dynasty, from 206 BC to AD 224, with the resulting compilation of the *Book* or *Record of Rites (Li Chi)* by Kuo Po. Kuo Po applied Feng Shui to the positioning of graves and in the later Sung dynasty (960 to AD 1279) Wang Chi applied it to house building.

To some, the one figure who was responsible for Feng Shui and its development to the point it has reached today was Yuen Kuen Chok who studied the art during the Tang dynasty (AD 618 to 906). He wrote much on the subject and laid the base of the practice as it is used now. There are also more recent published works such as the *Imperial Encyclopaedia (Ku Chin T'u Shu Chi Ch'eng)* of the eighteenth century. In China, Feng Shui was and is practised a great deal, save only for a comparatively brief and enforced break during the era of the Cultural Revolution.

Figure 1:
In Hong Kong, Primordial Pah Kwa is often placed over the front door to protect the house from harmful arrows of sha chi

The west has been relatively slow in taking up the philosophies and practice of Feng Shui. It was not until the late nineteenth century that some appreciation of the technique reached westerners, in the main through the visits and travels of missionaries. Until recently, Feng Shui was translated into English as 'Chinese Geomancy', a term which, although fairly accurate, covers just one dimension of a large and complex system.

Approaches to Feng Shui

There are several schools or approaches to Feng Shui that essentially are due to their place of origination. The first, the Form School, was developed by scholars who inhabited a region of China dominated by hills that provided a dramatic backdrop with impressive peaks and troughs. This approach dwelt upon the characteristics of the scenery and its different formations.

A little later, and in another area of China where there were no such mountains and hills, scholars applied Feng Shui to a very different landscape. The scenery was plain and flat and an altogether different approach had to be adopted. This led to a scheme based upon the points of the compass and so the Compass School was formed (sometimes also called the Fukien method). Many practitioners of Feng Shui now use a combination of these two working practices.

A third system has been used by some, although its basis is very much more tenuous than the other methods. It comprises a blend of sayings and folklore, observations and fabricated practices but nevertheless has been developed and used by some.

The scope of Feng Shui

Feng Shui is an all-encompassing approach to living and to ordering one's environment. It combines what at first seems a curious mix of factors:
- philosophy
- interior (and exterior) design
- divination
- plain common sense
- (and in some cases) astrology.

15

For many people it is the 'oracle' that should be consulted before many decisions are taken, and in China it often is the focus around which people live and how they plan their homes and lay them out internally. It can be used to choose the most opportune days upon which to start something, whether it be a marriage, building a new home, commencing a new business or starting a new job. It can even be used to decide the location of a relative's grave. It thus forms a predictive tool for life's situations, whether impending changes involve the individual, their family or their finances.

Feng Shui today

Hong Kong is a prime example of geographical conditions lending themselves to prosperity. The natural terrain of Hong Kong Island is widely regarded as providing good Feng Shui, with the high ground of the Peak to the rear and an unobstructed body of water, Victoria Harbour, to the front. Between the hills and the water lies Hong Kong's famous financial strip running from Central to Wanchai.

This physical landscape is complemented by modern technology and adherence to Feng Shui principles. Active, highrise cities tend to create a grid of energy that is both horizontal and vertical, with a reach of several miles – which many believe accounts for Hong Kong's buoyant economy, even in the wake of the 1997 Asian Crisis.

In Hong Kong, it would be a brave developer or town planner who drew up plans for a site without involving a Feng Shui master, or geomancer, in the consultation process. To combat negative or harmful chi, many apartments and office blocks are built with auspicious octagonal shaped rooms, others with round or mirror windows. In allocating floors and flats, most high rises 'miss out' the fourth floor because the number 'four' is pronounced in the same way as 'si' or death.

Hong Kong's skyline is dominated by examples of architectural principles subordinated to Feng Shui. One building even has a large hole through the centre to allow negative energy to pass without affecting the fortune of the occupants.

The Hong Kong & Shanghai Bank building in Central was constructed along Feng Shui lines and gained the approval of Feng Shui masters on its completion in 1985. As empty space in front of the main entrance is thought to promote financial success, the bank also bought the land opposite the building and donated it to the government on the basis that there should be nothing built there. Despite its angles and steel crosses, the nearby Bank of China building is regarded by many as a model of architectural Feng Shui, but the Hong Kong stock market crash in the early 1980s was attributed by some to its construction. While some say the Bank of China sends arrows of chi raining down on Government House below, many think the angles are offset by an overpass and network of roads which effectively embrace the building.

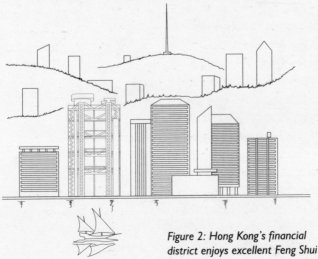

Figure 2: Hong Kong's financial district enjoys excellent Feng Shui

How to use this book

This book offers a quick, easy reference guide for readers who would like to apply Feng Shui to their home or office but do not have the time to study the subject in depth. It also provides, for those readers keen to enhance their understanding, broad coverage of the framework of beliefs that lie behind this ancient art. Thus the book is divided into two sections. Part I deals with the theory, from the basics of yin and yang through to trigrams and the I Ching. Part II is a survival kit for Feng Shui living, from garden design to room-by-room-analysis to enhancing health, money and romantic prospects.

Part I
Feng Shui:
The Theory

The Basics
of Feng Shui

One of the important components of Feng Shui is the theory of the five elements, which is considered later in this section. Other factors to be explained are yin and yang, chi and the concept of trigrams. Practitioners of Feng Shui regard their surroundings as an expression of chi and it is therefore appropriate to consider first the topic of chi, and Tao (pronounced to rhyme with cow) with which it is inextricably linked and from which Feng Shui is derived.

Tao

Early western proponents of Feng Shui found that Taoism was a religion and philosophical system well established in China. Taoism, otherwise known as the way (or the other way), existed alongside the established ideals of Confucianism and in some respects offered an alternative. The philosophy of Taoism was developed more than two thousand years ago from old traditions of foretelling and the worship of nature (one can readily see from this a clear link with Feng Shui). Scholars of the time include Laotzu who wrote the central Taoist text, the *Tao-te-Ching* and was often regarded as the founder of Taoism; and Chuang-tzu to whom was attributed the *Chuang-tzu*.

These philosophers helped to formulate the concept of Dao (or Tao) as the source of all creation as well as a code of behaviour for living in harmony with nature. Dao was considered to be the hidden impetus behind the enormously diverse happenings in the natural world. Followers based their spiritual life upon a combination of Dao and nature because they saw in nature a permanent and harmonious system creating a stable social order, far superior to that imposed by man and the powers of the state. Although Taoism can thus be seen to be fundamental to Chinese religious and philosophical life, Dao is not a God as it might seem from the perspective of other religions but a metaphysical concept.

Followers and teachers of Taoism conformed to this natural order of things, abandoning materialism and purposive action for simplicity; and showed great interest in issues relating to health, including herbal medicine and good diet. The individual is meant to fall into line with the way the universe works, the Tao, and, through following this path, ultimately accomplishes unity with the Tao. A further development of Tao was that its followers sought long life, if not immortality, through the use of magic and alchemy. While immortality was hardly possible, an overall system of hygiene was developed which is still used and which emphasises the need for regular breathing and concentration to confer long life and help prevent disease.

In the past, many Chinese would temporarily leave the bustle and pressures of life and return to nature, either in the countryside or at a mountain retreat. This allowed them to rest and be healed, and during this time they might paint, write poetry or perhaps compose music in an attempt to absorb the positive forces at the heart of nature itself. This practice also instilled in the Chinese a very positive approach to life itself, and an assertion of their health, well-being and vitality.

Some Taoists did indeed seek immortality through the use of herbs or chemicals, or even through the location of the 'isles of the immortals'. However, the majority were more often interested in the benefits of herbal medicine and pharmacology and it seems that they did much to advance these subjects. In addition they developed good diets and gymnastic and massage routines to help maintain the body's condition.

It can be seen quite readily that the principal aims of Feng Shui, arranging everything around us to generate greater harmony with the environment, do have much in common with the practice of Tao.

Chi

Chi, pronounced 'chee' and often spelled ch'i, is thought by the Chinese to be the most important aspect of Feng Shui. Chi encompasses everything and holds together all the different aspects and factors involved in Feng Shui. It is the energy and force that flows all around and within and accordingly is sometimes called the cosmic breath. Chi is basically the life force, giving life to everything whether it be the movement of the stars, the weather and the changing seasons or the spiritual and physical changes within ourselves. Chi cannot be seen, heard or felt; it does not register upon any of our senses. It is apparent merely by its effect. In essence it refers to beneficial currents, whether generated by a propitious environment or created by a well-ordered room with freely-flowing air.

A house situated on a particular site in a certain way will be subject to highly positive and beneficial chi (which itself creates a healthy environment) and, by generating a positive environment within the home, can also help to produce a prosperous life. The aim is to have the chi enter the site, and, after moving around gently, to have it leave at the other side. Within the house the chi should be allowed and encouraged to move in different ways, sometimes being slowed down, on other occasions accelerated. In a room where there is a lot happening, such as a general living room, the chi can be strengthened by reflection between mirrors. While in a room which is quieter, such as a bedroom or sitting room, it needs to be directed around the room in a peaceful way. The chi also needs an exit from the room which should be different from the entrance, so a room with just one door cannot allow chi to circulate and it will become a stagnant area.

Feng Shui is basically the arrangement of our immediate environment to enable us to benefit from the good effects of chi. Experts in the discipline of Feng Shui regard our surroundings as a representation and manifestation of chi. There are three main conditions or stages of chi – sheng chi, si chi and sha chi.

Sheng chi

Sheng chi means 'moving upward' and is a positive type of chi to be found in places that are bright, refreshing and uplifting. By extrapolation, people in these places are generally content and happy. Sheng chi is to be found by a wood, the sea, a park, a field or other naturally pleasant setting (*see*, for example, Figure 3). When an individual possesses sheng chi, they are full of hope and optimism. When the moon is near to its full phase, it is called sheng.

Figure 3: Site conducive to sheng chi. The house is protected by higher ground and trees to the north, and embraced by a stream to the south

Si chi

Si chi is the opposite of sheng chi – reducing, lessening or dying and has an overall negative impact. A location that is disorderly and decayed has si chi and in the environment around us si chi is reflected in sick animals, exhausted soil and therefore very poor vegetation. It is not surprising then that people are affected in a similar way, being sick, poorly and depressed. When the moon is almost new, it is said to be si.

Sha chi

Sha chi, or 'killing breath' as it is sometimes known, is a little different from sheng chi and si chi. It is harmful energy, the chi that is possessed when people are angry or when a place has a threatening or peculiar feel to it. Sha chi originates from negative surroundings both above and below ground and, depending upon its origin, can cause various detrimental effects. Sha chi from below the ground causes sickness and saps energy and so a person may feel tired and apprehensive for no obvious reason. This would certainly apply to a house built in a low, dank and possibly dark location. Beneficial chi is generally considered to move around in a gentle way, following a curving path, but sha chi travels in straight lines.

Sha chi emanating from above ground causes nervous complaints and illnesses. It may result in troubles in someone's personal life (such as a marriage breakdown) and financial concerns, whether personal or relating to business. Sha chi can affect houses in a number of ways, some of which will be mentioned later, but here are some examples.

It is well known that sha chi will affect a house detrimentally if the house is sited at a T-junction in the road or if a road or a river runs straight at or from one of the doors or windows (*see* Figure 4). Similarly, a house situated at the end of a cul-de-sac will receive harmful energy as will one that is built surrounded by other structures (bridges, roads or other buildings) which completely box it in.

Feng Shui

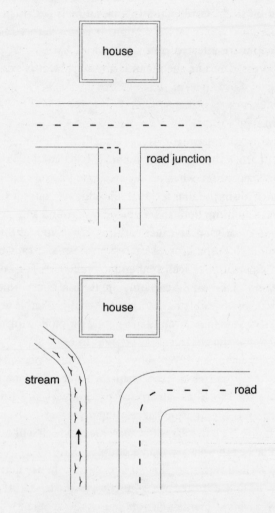

Figure 4: Sha chi will adversely affect houses sited in these positions

Other configurations that can create sha chi include:
- pointed objects aligned with the door or a window
- being opposite a ruined building
- a noisy neighbourhood

• overhead cables or wires obstructing the view
• proximity to a noisy building such as a fire station or
  a bar
• proximity to a graveyard.

Sha chi can also be generated inside a building by the positioning of furniture and style of decoration. This is a well known aspect of Feng Shui and is encountered in several instances later in the book. Let us consider these factors a little more.

Generation of sha chi

When a building is faced by the corner of another building, perhaps across the road, it will be subject to sha chi. This sha chi is often referred to as 'secret arrows' in which the arrow flies from the offending building, threatening the building or site in question. The effects can be varied, but may include the occupants being particularly prone to illnesses.

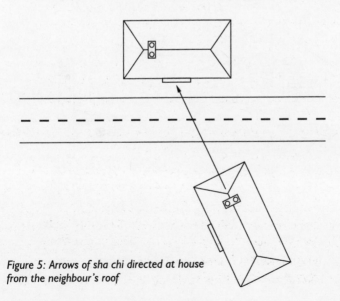

Figure 5: Arrows of sha chi directed at house
from the neighbour's roof

Whenever there is a building by a road or some other public way, the edge of that building will produce sha chi which may be directed at your house Figure 5).

The actual site upon which a house is built may also contribute to the sha chi. Within the ground itself, faults and similar features create sha chi. This may also include small valleys which if straight will generate sha chi. External, man-made features such as poles and wires, used for various reasons including the provision of the utilities, can also be detrimental because they carry sha chi.

Wires should preferably run at a low angle to the building, almost parallel to it, and poles, posts and trees should not be positioned immediately outside windows (Figure 6).

Figure 6: Arrows of sha chi directed at house from electricity pylon

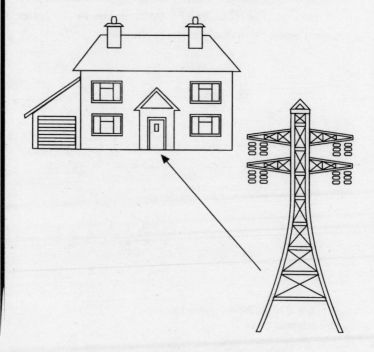

As will be discussed later, there are many configurations inside the house that should either be avoided or amended, to avoid or lessen the sha chi. For this reason, stairs should not descend immediately facing the outer door, and the back door of a house should not be visible when entering through the front door. In both cases good chi is allowed to flow directly out of the house before it has been able to circulate. It is also better to avoid a layout in which the house is split by a corridor at the centre. This may lead to a division of the house, which is a bad thing, and the corridor may encourage the chi to move too rapidly.

This brings us to the next factor involved in Feng Shui, which is to be considered before looking at the application of Feng Shui. In the flow of chi, there are negative and positive aspects, known as yin and yang, the subject of the next section.

Yin and Yang

Yin and yang are the be all and end all: the cause of life and death. The Chinese equate the earth, or creation with yin and the sky or heaven with yang. Pictorially, yin is represented by a line of two dashes while yang is a continuous line, each derived from the square and circle which in turn represent the earth and heaven, respectively (*see* Figure 7). The origin of this lies with the fact that yin and yang lines were used as ancient oracles. Oracles of ancient times gave a yes or no answer to any question put to them and yes was represented by the yang, unbroken, line and yin, no, by the broken line.

Figure 7

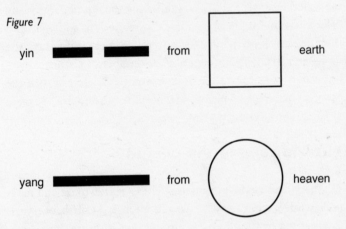

yin ▬ ▬ from   earth

yang ▬▬▬ from   heaven

Yin and yang are inextricably linked because while yin is restful and yang is active, activity invariably ends with rest and likewise rest leads to further activity. The activity of yang ends with the inactivity of yin. This is graphically shown in the well known symbol for yin and yang which is often called the T'ai ch'i, something quite different from the system of exercise for which the full name is T'ai chi chu'an (*see* Figure 8).

Although yin and yang are effectively opposites, together they produce a balance and within each there is some part of

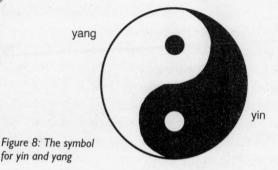

yang

yin

Figure 8: The symbol for yin and yang

the other, represented in the symbol by the dot of contrasting colour – white in black and black in white. Yin and yang and their negative/positive aspects also relate to the individual, the home and his or her occupation. A number of characteristics or properties can be attributed to yin or yang and in turn the physical makeup of a person will be one or the other. The table opposite shows some typical properties.

Yin and yang in the person

When applied to the personality, yin is gentle, quiet and magnetic while yang is fiery, active and intense. At birth, everyone is either yin or yang in their physical constitution. It is sometimes possible to determine which one you are by studying the features of your face with the aid of a mirror.

Physical features

The yin person has features that tend to be well-spaced and set apart from an imaginary line that bisects the head from chin to forehead. Thus their features may include a cleft at the end of the nose, a gap in the front teeth, eyes well set apart, a large mouth with full lips. Mild climates tend to generate this type of character.

Not unexpectedly, the yang person has facial features which tend to be concentrated nearer to the imaginary centreline. The eyes tend therefore to be closer set, the nose small and flat and the lower jaw is square set. This type of person is thought to come from climatic extremes, including the cold and mountainous areas.

Attributes

Each type of person can be related to the various attributes and therefore a yin person tends to reveal him or herself through thoughts and a typical occupation would be teaching, writing or research. The yang person uses actions to express him or herself and typical occupations would be sport, business, engineering and the armed services. However, it is perhaps obvious that a yin type may have a yang occupation and vice versa.

When a person considers what will be the ideal surroundings for them, it is necessary to accommodate the physical constitution and the occupation. For the former, a complementary environment is required and that means the opposite is needed; a yang person will need a predominantly yin milieu. The opposite then applies for a yin person. The surroundings should also be made to match your job so that if your occupation is yin, there should be a yin area to promote thought. These varying factors can be summarised as follows:

Physical Constitution	Occupation	Nature of Surroundings	Special area required
yin	yin	mainly yang	yin
yin	yang	almost exclusively yang	
yang	yang	mainly yin	yang
yang	yin	almost exclusively yin	

This type of analysis provides a quick guideline for arranging our individual environment. This theme will be developed in later sections.

The five elements

As already mentioned, the five elements are another important aspect of chi and therefore Feng Shui. The five elements are wood, metal, fire, water and earth. Many different oriental philosophies and medical practices are based upon the essential structure of the five elements. Each element confers certain characteristics upon the nature and personality of the individual and, in addition, there are typical associations when it comes to attitudes, occupations, likes and dislikes. It is actually considered beneficial to have some of each element in your overall personality as this confers a balance to the individual and it is useful when it comes to the application of Feng Shui. These elements are not related in any way to the astrology studied and practised in the west; they are essentially all part of the makeup of the character of an individual.

Individuals are considered to have some part of each element in their makeup, but the particular characteristics of one element are shown more strongly than the others and dominate the overall disposition. Each element is now considered with its dominant characteristics and associations and it may be possible to recognise in yourself the dominant element of your makeup.

Wood

Otherwise known as *Mu*, the pioneer, wood brings its natural properties to the individual. It is strong, often pliable and can take a lot of strain. It has roots which usually go very deep into the ground providing sustenance and stability. In addition it

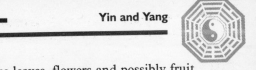

Figure 9:
The symbol
for wood

produces leaves, flowers and possibly fruit that are, of course, seeds that are spread for the perpetuation of the species.

Rectangular, upright shapes are associated with wood, whether it be tall buildings or steep-sided hills. Interior design corresponding to this element would be of an essentially rectangular pattern. Green and blue is the colour associated with this element, apart from dark blues which fit elsewhere. Spring is the season of wood and anyone born in this season (roughly from the beginning of February to the beginning of May) is optimistic and bursting with ideas. Some of the other aspects of character corresponding to this element are given opposite.

Illness may result from imbalances and in the case of this element, typical complaints would include pains in the back, irritability, indecision, liver and gall bladder ailments, weakness or paralysis of the limbs, and eye problems. These reflect the parts of the body that tend to be linked with wood and hence the areas that suffer when there is a disparity.

Wood

Positive Attributes	Negative Attributes
active	anger
practical	(should avoid wind)
likes to win	
can be domineering	
demonstrative	
busy	
kind and friendly	
generous	
romantic	
good co-ordinator	

Certain occupations are allied more with wood than the other elements. These include many of the creative vocations such as writing, painting, photography, music and interior design. These professions clearly exemplify the creative nature of such individuals. In addition, occupations relating to architecture and the landscape would not be uncommon.

In the home it is important that there is a quiet corner for contemplation and creation, whether it be composing music, drawing, painting or simply reading.

Metal

Metal is the catalyst, *Chin*, and is considered to strengthen. It is also very workable and versatile and is used in a whole host of objects for both everyday, functional use from vehicles and machines to wire and computers and in items of great beauty such as jewellery.

The shapes associated with metal are the round and the oval which are reflected in the land by way of rounded hills and in buildings through the use of domes and similar structures. Interior themes comprise regular, rounded shapes and patterns and the colours of metal are typically white, grey, silver or similar. Autumn is the season corresponding with metal and those born in the period from early August to early November could well be the type who want everything just so – perfectionists. In addition to liking order and justice, other attributes are:

Figure 10: The symbol for metal

Metal

Positive Attributes	Negative Attributes
organised	inflexible
severe	sorrow
likes to control	(should avoid dryness)
exact	
appreciates quality	
moral	
wants to be right	

Diseases of the large intestine and lungs and other conditions relating to the spine and also depression are possible results of an imbalance of metal.

The attributes of metal that relate, among others, to order and organisation find a suitable outlet in occupations such as the police or armed forces, the arts, the legal profession, computing and certain branches of engineering. The home should be tidy and well organised with a corner set aside for contemplative thought.

Fire

Known as the magician, *Huo*, fire is obviously full of life and brightness and is hot and dry. Hot deserts naturally fall under its control.

The fundamental shape of fire is considered to be an elongated triangle which is reflected in nature by jagged, pointed hills and mountains and in man-made features by pointed spires and roofs. Designs inside buildings would incorporate

Figure 11: The symbol for fire

bright, cheery patterns possibly with a radiating theme. As would be expected, the colours associated with this element include all shades of red and also purple. The colour red is thought to be very propitious be it only red bricks, or red paving stones in a path. Summer is the season associated with fire and anyone born between early May and early August will be full of vitality. Other characteristics of this element include:

Fire

Positive Attributes	Negative Attributes
courageous	rashness
perceptive	impulsiveness
courteous	(should avoid heat)
charitable	
communicative	
likes excitement	
loving	
dislikes boredom	

There are many conditions and illnesses that can result from a disproportion of fire. Heart disease, circulatory problems (such as high blood pressure), muscular and digestive complaints are all likely, as is emotional upset and similar ailments where the origin lies with matters of the heart.

Occupations that readily match individuals covered by this element include any profession in which fire is involved and also those of a mathematical or numerical nature (accounting, for example) and those involving modern technology, such as computing and electronics. The home of such people should ideally be, and it is often the case, a warm welcoming environment suitable for receiving visitors but also for private moments which are greatly treasured.

Water

Known as the philosopher, *Shui*, water is the element that cleanses and rejuvenates – the very source of life. Flowing water follows its course naturally till it finds its way to the ocean. All areas where water is found, by seas, rivers and also by man-made waterways are influenced by this element.

The colours associated with water are dark shades – black, navy blue and similar. The wave form is the basic shape associated with water and this becomes undulating, rolling countryside on land. Internal themes follow this shape with flowing designs and surfaces. Winter is the time of year linked with water and anyone born between early November and early February will have a very emotional aspect to their character but will quite often cover up their feelings. Other characteristics of this element are shown in the table below.

Water	
Positive Attributes	*Negative Attributes*
honest	fear
imaginative	can be secretive
wise	(should avoid cold)
ambitious	
independent	
innovative	
intelligent	

Illnesses due to a imbalance of water include nervous problems such as phobias, depression and lethargy; circulatory conditions such as low or high blood pressure; arthritis and other diseases of the joints and certain digestive ailments.

Professions that can be linked to water, in addition to anywhere water is used, are those which incorporate transport and commerce in general or involve communication. Furthermore, a number of complementary medical therapies and working with pharmaceuticals also correspond to water. In the home, the emotional aspects of the character of the individual should be matched by a place that can easily be made private and quiet.

Figure 13: The symbol for earth

Earth

As will be shown later, earth, the diplomat, *T'u*, is in a way central to everything else as it is the element that holds all the other elements. In its simplest form it is the ground or soil that not only enables life to grow but also takes back the dead organisms and recycles them into new life. It represents a complete balance.

Not surprisingly, the colours connected with earth are browns, yellows and oranges and the fundamental shape is essentially a planar surface i.e. flat land with broad buildings with square elevations. Unlike the other elements, there is no particular time of year that is strongly linked with earth. However, it is sometimes associated with the summer, at the end of the season for fire, around early August. Those born at this time tend to be kind-hearted and caring and helpful towards others. Further characteristics associated with this element include:

Earth

Positive Attributes	Negative Attributes
honest	worry
patient	can be stubborn
gregarious	(should avoid damp)
loyal	
sympathetic	
compassionate	
punctilious	
likes to be needed	

Typical ailments connected with an imbalance of earth affect primarily the stomach and pancreas, and create certain nervous disorders. These include digestive problems which may involve conditions such as anorexia, diabetes, anxiety, insecurity and confusion.

Occupations that match individuals under this element include charitable work and health care. The various aspects of construction (foundations, tunnelling, building in general) in which there is a very close involvement with the ground are also appropriate as are the financial service sectors of banking, investments and related activities. The home revolves around providing comfort, whether it is in the kitchen, dining room or lounge.

Interaction between the five elements

Identifying your own element and that of your partner and children can lead to a greater understanding of personal relationships and may help to avoid or resolve domestic difficulties that arise. It can also be useful when choosing and setting out a home.

It has to be appreciated that each of the five elements relates to the others and has a certain interaction with them. Some practitioners of Feng Shui call this the three cycles; these are the cycles of generation, destruction and mitigation (or moderation). The cycles are presented in simple terms below:

Generation cycle	Destruction cycle
earth supports metal	earth absorbs water
metal contains water	water extinguishes fire
water supplies wood	fire melts metal
wood feeds fire	metal cuts wood
fire helps earth	wood hinders earth

These inter-relationships can be represented graphically and by doing so the cycle of mitigation or moderation becomes clear (*see* Figure 14). This means that one of the elements has a moderating influence on two others that are interacting. For example, and consulting the diagram, it can be seen that wood moderates the interaction between water and fire. In each case, the moderator lies between the two elements that are conflicting.

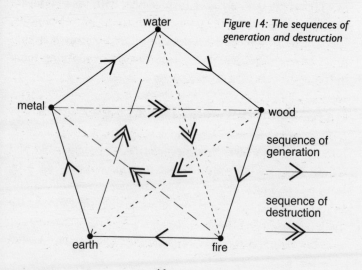

Figure 14: The sequences of generation and destruction

sequence of generation

sequence of destruction

In summary:

Moderation cycle
wood moderates between water and fire
fire moderates between wood and earth
earth moderates between fire and metal
metal moderates between earth and water
water moderates between metal and wood

The relevance of these interactions and the benefit of appreciating them comes to the fore later in our study when the element for an individual can be matched with compass directions (and their appropriate elements) to select suitable colours etc. to create the most harmonious situation possible.

Significance of the five elements

Each of the five elements is shown in the landscape by particular features of land forms and in the environment created by man, through the various shapes of buildings. Referring back to the personal attributes listed previously and linking this to the properties and features described in this section allows, amongst other things, guidance to be drawn on the suitability of buildings for professions. In each case, the aspects that each element symbolises forms the basis for the analysis. Thus, for example, wood is shown in the earlier analysis to represent creativity, lots of ideas and to be associated with professions that utilise these qualities (*see* The five elements/Wood, page 38). This picture is reinforced by the details that follow on pages 48–50:

Wood
This is represented by structures that resemble the upright shape of trees. So in the natural landscape, high, steep-sided

47

hills (but not with pointed peaks) fall into this group. Within the built environment, one naturally thinks of skyscrapers, blocks of flats, large factory chimneys and similar features. Such shapes are in the main of recent origin, reflecting more modern techniques of construction. However, a building that does not necessarily comply with the wood shape but is constructed out of wood, could fall within this category.

Buildings falling within the scope of this element are taken to be associated with creation and growth. This means that professions and businesses such as those in the care sector, catering, and in creative areas, would ideally be housed in buildings within this element. Perhaps the most obvious occupation to pursue in a 'wood building' would be the manufacture of wooden items, be they pieces of furniture or handmade toys.

Metal

Metal is taken to be reflected in rounded features which in the landscape are rounded, dome-shaped hills and in buildings, anything with a domed appearance, a feature that is becoming more prevalent in some sectors of modern architecture, as well as being found in the architecture of the past. Arches and circular features would also be included in this category, and in the main, buildings with such features tend to be rather special: large buildings intended for the gathering of many people, or for ceremonies whether state or civic.

Buildings with this sort of structure are ideal for ventures and businesses of a financial nature as metal has a natural association with money. In addition, manufacturing with metal, and the sale of items associated with metal (such as jewellery) are readily included in this element. However, because metal is also the material from which weapons are made, it can represent aggression, in business for example. In this case it is important that the surroundings belong to a complementary element.

Fire

The flames within a fire are usually represented as flickering, stretched out, triangular shapes with points. Thus in the natural environment, fire is shown in pointed mountain tops although it need not necessarily just be found on mountains. Buildings that reflect this shape clearly include churches and temples that have steep spires, towers or similar features. There are also many other buildings with towers or steep roofs that can be taken to represent fire. Indeed, many domestic houses have roofs with quite a steep pitch which may be taken to represent fire. Any connection with learning, such as schools and libraries, would benefit from a building with a fire shape in some aspect of its design.

Water

Water is rather different from the other elements because its shape is determined by the shape of the container in which it is held. However, it is generally accepted that it possesses a curved if irregular form which in the landscape is represented by hills that roll gently and are without any definite trend in their shape, that is, they do not form a chain or a definite circular shape. When it comes to buildings, this category may be more difficult to qualify. In some respects it can end up as the miscellaneous of all the elements, because buildings with strange or complex shapes are included, although they should have a soft, rounded outline. A lot of modern architecture uses vast expanses of glass in buildings and this is also taken to represent water. However, it is preferable that the glass be used with wood and/or metal as they are part of the sequence of generation outlined in Figure 14.

Looking back to the characteristics associated with this element, we can see intelligence, innovation, imagination and ambition which, with a natural tendency for communication, points clearly to the performing arts for buildings within this element. In addition, other suitable professions include the media and computing.

Earth

By comparison with hills and mountains, the earth is relatively flat and so features such as plains and plateaux are included. Low hills that maintain a flat profile would also be considered as a feature of this element, as would some mountains with extensive flat summits. When considering buildings, this element is obviously represented by those with flat roofs of which there are many examples – office blocks, apartments and so on. In addition, because an enormous number of buildings are made, in part or whole, with bricks and/or concrete, they will show some qualities of the earth element even if other features suggest an influence from another element. In addition to the construction activities mentioned earlier (*see* The five elements/Earth, page 44) farming has a natural association with this element.

Matching buildings with locations

Each of these five elements has a significance in two ways. Firstly the building may belong to a particular element and then the building may be situated in a location that has the same or a different elemental association. The implications for each type of building (i.e. each element) are now considered briefly within the five different locations available (wood, fire, etc).

Wood

Bear in mind the typical immediate environment of this element, whether urban or rural. A building within the element wood will clearly be well suited to a wood environment; the latter may be other wooden buildings, trees or tall tree-like buildings. This is a good and reliable set up. When the wood building is in a location that is essentially metal in its characteristics, there is the potential for conflict and ill-fortune. From the sequence of destruction (*see* Figure 14) we can see that metal destroys wood so a wood building in metal surroundings is likely to have a negative influence on the resident business and/or people. This may show in physical injury or commercial problems – in effect the building would end up giving to the surroundings. The converse is true of a wood building in a fire location. Fire is fed by wood, in other words the occupation carried out in the building would have a net loss, although not in a negative way. Buildings which naturally house a function that gives something to an area include hospitals. As with the wood/metal combination, this would not be such a good location for a business due to the net loss which would be experienced.

The combination of a wood-element building in a water-element location is very good because water is linked to wood in the sequence of generation (*see* Figure 14). This means that the one feeds the other and the implication is that whatever activity is housed in the building, it will flourish. When situated in an earth-element location, a wood building has the potential to be quite productive. The earth feeds the wood, but can only do so for a limited time so it would be necessary to compensate for this in some way.

Metal

Because of the specific characteristics (domes, arches, etc.) of the form of the building in the metal element, it is not the natural choice for many people when considering what type of building to erect. A metal-element building in a metal-element location is consequently not particularly common. If it does occur, the activity carried out within the building should not conflict with the general activities of the area. Metal destroys wood, thus a metal-element building in a wood-element location could dominate the surroundings leading not only to financial success but even to exploitation. Conversely, fire destroys metal and so a commercial enterprise would be wise to avoid this combination.

Metal generates water, thus a metal-element building in a water-element location will result in an outpouring of finance to the surroundings. Such a location would therefore be unsuitable for a bank or similar business but may be acceptable to an organisation such as a media company or possibly some sort of religious centre that benefits from its product naturally finding an effective channel to the outside world. Finally, in an earth-element location, a metal building would be the focus of success, because earth generates metal. This would be ideal for any business, particularly if the building incorporated some circular features or domes.

Fire

The fire location – with mountain peaks or their urban equivalent, steep roofs and buildings with sharp corners – seems to imply a continual restlessness. Although a building and location from this same element can be steady, the need for excitement (*see* The five elements/Fire, page 41) means that it will only be productive for a limited time. For a business, therefore, it may be a good place to start but there will always be the need to contemplate moving.

An especially good combination is that of a fire-element building in a wood-element location. This is because wood feeds fire and therefore the local surroundings help sustain the business in the fire-element building. The same will apply to a home – and prosperity can be expected from this combination. From the earlier sequence (*see* Figure 14 on page 46) we can see that fire destroys metal and so a fire-element building in a metal-element location will be dominant and this combination should lead to success, whether financial or personal. Thus if there is the potential to move your business to a building with steep roofs and other angular features at a location with a predominance of domes, arches etc, then it could be your key to success! The exact opposite is true of the fire building in a water location, because water puts out fire and this would not be a very auspicious place to start a business. The water may be represented by natural water as in streams and lakes or manmade watersides as found at the docks or by canals. Buildings at a water-element location would have a strange shape with no set pattern and rounded edges.

Finally, fire generates earth (as represented by the ashes left after the fire) and so this combination is a good one. A fire-element building will be readily seen in an earth element location and will be something of a focal point and will be beneficial for the area. A good example of such a building in this area would be a hospital or community centre. A business would do well enough, but perhaps more importantly, it would be a beneficiary to the community.

Water

Buildings that fall under this element are, as stated above, irregular in shape, often with a lot of glass in their construction. They tend not to be symmetrical as with many other buildings and often show flowing lines. This means that the water-element type of building is not seen very often. Although the water-element location can be represented by rolling hills, it usually refers directly to a body of water nearby. This combination would be quite good as it confers constancy while allowing changes to occur – thus adapting to changing circumstances. A water-element building in a wood-element location would be subject to the relationship between the elements, that is, the water would feed the wood. Such a building would therefore be better put to a community use. A similarly beneficial result, although at more of a personal level, would be a water-element building in a metal-element location. This is because metal generates water, resulting in a continued flood of good things with the resultant spin-off being prosperity and well-being.

A less propitious combination would be that of a water-element building in a fire-element location. In physical terms the water type of building would not mix well with buildings of the fire type and in Feng Shui terms the water would destroy the fire. This would almost certainly result in friction as the occupants of the water-element building became dominant in the area, thus antagonising neighbours. This would happen however justified or unjustified the neighbours were. Because earth destroys water, an earth-element type of location would not be a good choice for a water-element building. The water would be soiled by the earth leading possibly to tarnished reputations and generally negative influences.

Earth

Although many buildings are made of brick and/or concrete and therefore have some link with the earth element, it is more the shape of the building than the materials of which it is built that matter. Thus a low perspective building with a flat roof would be typical. In an earth-element location, such a building provides a rock-steady base but one from which there are unlikely to be many earth-shattering developments. That, however, might suit a great many people! Wood 'destroys' the earth (taking nourishment from it) and so although this arrangement (earth-element building in wood-element location) may at first sight seem acceptable, in fact it will lead to a depletion of resources, both personal and financial and should not be endured for too long.

Because earth generates metal, an earth-element building in a metal-element location should again be the sort of building that houses an activity of benefit to the community. There would be a continual outpouring of resources that would not suit a business or anyone who needed to save their meagre funds. The opposite is true of a earth-element building in a fire-element location; fire generates earth and therefore this creates a positive effect for those living or working in this set-up. Not only that, the combination is ongoing and productive and so would lend itself to almost any type of use. In a water element location, the earth-element building benefits from the dominance of earth over water but the water location will suffer. Thus success may come at the expense of those nearby or the environment.

Moderating elemental conflicts

When a building, be it house, office or factory, of a particular element type is located in an area under another element, and one which will confer a negative influence, it is possible to offset the bad influence by use of one of the remaining elements. This is based upon the cycle of moderation mentioned earlier (*see* Interaction between the five elements, page 45) and an example would be:

Using wood
Wood moderates between fire and water. So if a fire element building were located in a water-element area – not a good combination as explained above – it would be possible to ame-

liorate the situation by introducing wood which supports fire because wood feeds fire. An alternative would be to introduce earth which destroys water. In each such case, there would be a moderating factor which either generates the element being destroyed or destroys the element that is threatening.

The moderating factor can be represented in many different ways from something simple such as an aquarium to introduce water to something more complex, perhaps introducing wood into the fire/water situation mentioned above such that the wood feeds the fire. In a practical way this could involve the use of the colour associated with wood (green or blue, but not dark blue), introduction of wood inside the building by means of screens, decorations or even just more wooden items such as furniture or surrounds. Outside the building, trees could be planted in strategic places, but it would be necessary to ensure this was done correctly (that is, do not plant to the south or outside windows) as mentioned elsewhere in this book.

We shall now consider briefly the moderating influence of the remaining elements, as specified earlier in the text, and provide general guidance on how this can be achieved. The relationships can be appreciated simply and graphically by consulting Figure 14.

Using fire

Fire moderates between wood and earth. Wood hinders earth but fire helps earth, so the introduction of a fire-related element will support earth. Fire can be introduced in many ways. Firstly, if considering the interior layout of a house, a nice open fire could be all that is required. Fire is also represented by the colour red and so the use of this colour in the decoration or in carpets, curtains or borders would all help in this situation. Externally there is less that can be done. Because fire is represented by spires, towers and steep roofs, it is unlikely that a building will be modified to the extent of changing the roof. If an extension is being added to the house, or a garage being constructed, then a pitched roof would be the obvious choice in this respect.

Using earth

Earth moderates between fire and metal. Of course fire melts metal, so because earth supports metal (and fire helps earth) this is the ideal moderating influence. The same applies where water extinguishes fire – because earth absorbs water. This situation may be represented by a metal-element building (rounded form) in a fire-element location (sharp hills or mountains; or steep roofed buildings and tower blocks etc.). Introducing earth can be achieved by introducing the material itself by means of a small construction – whether a wall, decorative tiles, or the use of an appropriate colour which in this case may be a brown, yellow or orange.

Using metal

Metal moderates between earth and water. Looking once more at the sequences of generation and destruction, we see that earth destroys water. However, metal generates water (*see* Figure 14) so this is the moderating influence. Metal can also moderate between earth and wood, when earth is threatened by wood because metal cuts wood. Inside a building, metal can be introduced quite simply and in a number of ways. The material itself can be used, perhaps by means of some wrought iron or through the strategic placing of a set of candlesticks. (If fire is also required, then this is the standard way of introducing both elements – candlesticks and candles.) Internal decoration can be altered to use the colours of metal which are white, grey, silver and similar. Externally it may be feasible to erect railings around a garden, a metal archway over which plants can trail, or if the budget can extend to it (or if you are a sculptor) to place a metal sculpture in the garden. This type of solution would be particularly appropriate to a water-element building in an earth-element location.

Using water

Water moderates between metal and wood. As you will no doubt appreciate by now, metal destroys wood – it cuts it and therefore water has to be introduced because water supports wood. Water can also be used as a moderating influence when fire and metal are in conflict. Fire melts metal, but of course water extinguishes fire. It is relatively straightforward to introduce water to a location. Internally this can be achieved by installing an aquarium, probably a better solution than adopting the colours of water which are dark blues, black, etc. It is unlikely that you will wish to paint your walls or ceiling in such dark colours, but this could be managed by the introduction of dark panels on doors, using a dark border on the walls or by placing a dark blue rug in the appropriate place. As already mentioned, a dark rug can be taken to represent a body of water and is a simple way of bringing water into the situation.

If the building is a commercial premises then it may be possible to introduce water by means of a fountain or even a small pond with fish, probably in the entrance area. Outside, whether considering domestic or commercial premises, it is much easier to construct a fountain, pond, or to utilise a stream.

These are merely some basic suggestions to indicate the sort of approach to be adopted when some moderating influence is required. As already stated, quite often a combination of influences is required but this can be achieved quite easily, as shown by the example of candles and candlestick. Another common solution is to have an aquarium and red fish when fire and water elements are necessary. In many cases, the item can be something simple and ordinary. Here are some other combinations that may prove useful, but this is only an indication, the list is certainly not exhaustive:

Combination of elements required	Possible solution
fire and metal	candles and candlestick
	stoves of various descriptions
wood and metal	metal chairs with wooden arms, etc.
	wrought iron trellis painted green or blue (the colour for wood)
	a metal tool with a wooden handle
wood and earth	a display of dried flowers in a stoneware vase
	a wooden framed painting with autumnal colours
water and fire	candles floating on water
wood and fire	an open log fire with log stack
	a wooden screen with red details/picture
earth and metal	small indoor garden in a metal trough
	ornaments of metal coloured in earth colours (gold, brass, or another metal painted appropriately)
water and wood	wooden ornament painted in the colours of water
	aquatic plant

A Broader
Perspective

Before turning to the workings and applications of Feng Shui it is interesting to note another aspect of the subject that is an extension of the pictorial representation of yin and yang. This is the concept of trigrams and their use in the presentation of the seasons and compass directions. It should be stated here that practitioners of Feng Shui quite often work in ways that are slightly different from each other. This is quite normal and to be expected, but some aspects of the subject may therefore differ between experts. Some incorporate a significant amount of astrology into their application of Feng Shui, others do not, while others place considerable emphasis on the use of trigrams, hexagrams and the link between Feng Shui and the *I Ching* (the *Book Of Changes*). In this book, a straightforward and relatively simple, descriptive account is presented to enable the reader to grasp the basics. Anyone who then wishes to delve more deeply into the subject can do so by means of the many sources now available.

Seasons and trigrams

Trigrams and I Ching
Developing from the use of yin and yang lines of the oracle, it became necessary to provide a greater flexibility and differentiation other than just yes and no. By combining the two lines to give all available permutations, four pairs of lines were produced (*as in* Figure 15) and later a third line was added to give the eight symbols, called trigrams (*see* Figure 16). These trigrams symbolised all that happens in earth and heaven and they were all thought to be constantly changing into each other thus representing the continual and transitional state of affairs in the real world. Each trigram has a particular name relating to natural processes in the world as listed on the next page (*also refer to* Figure 16, page 65):

Figure 15

North	Winter
South	Summer
East	Spring
West	Autumn

K'un — Earth – the opposite to Ch'ien; it signifies passive, feminine, kindness and devotion

Ch'ien — Heaven – creatively inspired with strength and vitality but also power, domination and coldness

Li — Fire – represents beauty and enlightenment and also clinging

K'an — Water – signifies deep thought and concentration and also danger

Chen — Thunder – this relates to movement and represents growth, being impulsive

Tui — Marsh – represents growth, joy, success and sensual pleasure

Ken — Mountain – represents calm, caution and thoroughness

H'sun (or sun) — Wind – signifies growth and animal life, flexibility

Figure 16: The eight trigrams used in I Ching and Feng Shui

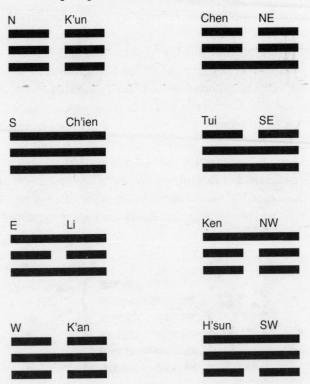

The eight trigrams are further classified into major and minor trigrams based upon the combination of their lines, yang being strong and yin being yielding. The categories are as follows:

major yang trigrams – Ch'ien and Tui
major yin trigrams – K'un and Ken
minor yang trigrams – K'an and H'sun
minor yin trigrams – Chen and Li

As will be appreciated, each trigram has a particular characteristic, thus heaven is creative and is yang. Different meanings are also attributed to the trigrams with respect to the natural phenomena in the world. Different trigrams are also associated with the different roles of family members. The table opposite lists the trigrams and their main associations.

The eight primary trigrams in combination generate the sixty-four (eight times eight) hexagrams of the I Ching. Each hexagram (*see* Figure 17) is thus composed of an upper and lower trigram, but in addition the internal trigrams (i.e. lines 2, 3 and 4, and 3, 4 and 5 from the top. Lines are counted 1–6 from bottom to top) which are called the nuclear trigrams. The analysis of these trigrams is the key to the study of I Ching.

Figure 17: A typical hexagram

The sixty four hexagrams are thus made up of the combinations of the two primary trigrams (*see* table opposite).

Each number can be looked up in a book on the I Ching to provide a full analysis. Each hexagram is interpreted to assist the individual who is consulting the I Ching to gain guidance. Below is one such example for hexagram 7, Shih, The Army.

Hexagram 7
Component trigrams: Primary: K'un (upper); K'an (lower); Nuclear: K'un (above); Chen (below)

The main associations of the eight trigrams

Name	Ch'ien	K'un	Chen	K'an	Ken	H'sun	Li	Tui
Means	heaven	earth	thunder	water	mountain	wind	fire	marsh
Traits	creative/ strong	receptive/ yielding	arousing/ moving	danger	resting	gentle	separate	joyful
Animal	horse	cow	dragon	pig	dog	cat	bird	sheep
Season	early winter	early autumn	spring	winter	early spring	early summer	summer	autumn
Polarity	yang	yin	yang	yang	yang	yin	yin	yin
Element	metal	soil	grass	wood	stone	air	fire	flesh
Direction	NW	SW	E	N	NE	SE	S	W
Family	father	mother	first son	middle son	third son	first daughter	second daughter	third daughter
Colour	purple	black	orange	red	green	white	yellow	blue
Part of Body	head	solar plexus	foot	ear	hand	thighs	eye	mouth

Keywords: Earth, water, firmness, authority, group action, danger, dissension, devotion

Commentary: There is a lack of harmony in your present situation, with contending forces causing confusion and unrest. But if you show firmness of purpose and keep your eye steadily on a goal which is worthy of attainment then you will succeed. Your exemplary action will transform aimless confusion into co-ordination and a worthwhile sense of direction. You will be an inspiration and a guide to others and will command their respect and admiration. With their help and support you will attain a position of distinction.

Judgement: With firmness and correctness and a leader of age and experience, there will be good fortune and no error.

A group of soldiers requires a steady and competent leader to unite them and keep them in good order. The leader must eliminate grievance and injustice and ensure instead that justice and peaceful concord prevail in the group. In and through this leadership endeavour he will command the respect, loyalty and love of his soldiers. The implication is that you should recruit the enthusiastic help and support of those around you to work together for a worthwhile common goal.

Interpretation: The only solid line in the hexagram is found in the middle line of the lower primary trigram. This gives rise to the image of a general who is the commander of the broken yin lines. This hexagram is about proper discipline, good order and legitimate and worthy power. It shows that an effective army requires effective soldiers and leadership. The good army remains in a state of prepared readiness until action is necessary, when it responds with spirit and alacrity. In a situation of conflict there is always the possibility of civil insurrection, but if the people are treated properly they will contribute to the size of the army.

Image: Water in the midst of the earth. The wise ruler nourishes and educates the people and collects from among them the multitude of his army. A ruler must instil a respect and desire for justice, good authority and harmony in his people by his own merits and example, commanding love and respect for his kindness, strength and unstinting support.

Line readings: *Line 1*: The army goes forth according to the proper rules. If these are not good there will be misfortune. (Success depends on the right motivation and the best preparation. Take a good and honest look at yourself.)

Line 2: The leader is in the middle of the army. There will be good fortune and no error. The king has thrice conveyed to him the orders of his favour. (You are awarded a distinction which is merited by the respect those around you have for your good judgement and successful work. They share in the credit and honour, as you all work together in a situation of mutual respect.)

Line 3: The army may have many inefficient leaders. There will be misfortune. (Be honest and vigilant about your faults and weaknesses otherwise your endeavour will end in failure. Maintain a perceptive and judicious sense of authority and control over yourself and others.)

Line 4: The army is in retreat. There is no error. (Now is the time to make a tactical retreat from a situation. You are not capitulating but surviving to fight again another day. Wait until a more advantageous time arrives. Be patient.)

Line 5: There are birds in the fields which it will be advantageous to seize and destroy. There will be no error. If the oldest son leads the army, and younger men idly occupy offices assigned to them, then however firm and correct he may be, there will be misfortune. (Success requires maturity. You must compensate for the immaturity of yourself and your advisers by seeking out those who can give wise and mature guidance. Guard against the mistake of confusing age with wisdom.)

Line 6: The king gives his rewards, appointing some to be rulers of states, and others to undertake the leadership of clans; but small men should not be employed. (You have achieved success but don't bask unthinkingly in your moment of glory. You should take time to survey and assess the nature and merits of your attainment with a scrupulous honesty. Ask yourself if you are where you deserve to be and where you want to be, and whether you are better, morally and practically, than the person you have replaced. Be true to yourself.

The I Ching is consulted by phrasing a question, which must be serious and genuine in nature, and which requires a yes or no response. The significance of the hexagrams rests with their symbolism and interpretation. Each represents a transitional state in life and all the hexagrams together represent a sequence of situations in life. Within the hexagram itself, it is the modification and movement of the yin and yang lines that change one hexagram into another.

Each hexagram has a Chinese name and a translation and its analysis falls into three categories: the Judgement, the Image, Line Readings and the Interpretation. The Judgement presents the overall theme and meaning of the hexagram with its good or bad fortune. The Image looks at the symbolic nature of the hexagram and the analysis of each individual line. (In these hexagrams, only the lines that are termed 'moving lines' are important – any text on I Ching will provide a full explanation.) The Interpretation gives an explanatory account of the Judgement and the structure of the hexagram. Each hexagram is preceded by a Commentary which summarises the overall meaning.

Origin of the trigrams

The trigrams are believed to have been created by the first Chinese emperor, Fu His, around 3000 BC. He was a teacher and a scholar and it is thought to have been his life's work. The work of Fu His was expanded and rearranged some 2,000 years later by the founder of the Chou dynasty, King Wen. At about this time, King Wen and his son the Duke of Chou expanded the trigrams into the six line hexagrams. A particular name was given to each hexagram and information was provided for each one, giving advice and a commentary which was known as the *T'uan* or the *Judgement*. There is also text (called the *Hsiang Chuan* or *Image*) based upon the lines of each hexagram and probably much of the text came from a number of authors.

In the early fifth century, further commentaries were added and this has continued over history, notably by the philosopher Chu His during the Sung dynasty (960–1279). The I Ching first reached the west in the early 1700s but a German missionary, Richard Wilhelm, discovered it in China in the late nineteenth century and after translation into German, it formed the basis for subsequent English translations.

Trigrams in Feng Shui

Feng Shui uses the basic linear representations of yin and yang, and the trigrams, although the names and interpretations may differ a little. Commencing with the broken and solid lines of yin and yang two further designs were generated to represent east and west. As we have already seen, yin stands for north and yang for south. Because yang is sun, light, heaven and all things that tend upwards, yang and south are portrayed as being to the top, thus where we in the west would expect north to be uppermost, in the case of Feng Shui it is the opposite. By using combinations of the two basic symbols, the four new designs can now be allocated to the compass points and the seasons, as shown. Figure 15 shows their configuration, and in each case the design is a different combination of the lines for yin and yang. By developing this system one stage further, adding a third line as described above, another four designs are created which represent the remaining compass points, north east, south west and so on (*as shown in* Figure 16, page 65). There are now eight symbols, the trigrams, each of which is made up of the characteristic three parallel lines or broken lines, and again the third line added is the line either for yin or yang. Each of the three-lined symbols or trigrams has some significance. In Feng Shui, the top line is the yin or yang, the earth and sky; the central line is the four seasons and points of the compass; the lowest line then represents man.

Each of the trigrams is given a name which is very similar to that described above for the I Ching, and thus each one then has a name, direction and also a trait or representation.

Direction	Name	Season	Representation
North	K'un (Responsive)	Winter	creation
North west	Ken (Calm)		mountain
West	K'an (Hazardous)	Autumn	moon
South west	H'sun (Wind)		gentle
South	Ch'ien (Inventive)	Summer	heaven
South east	Tui (Lake)		joy
East	Li (Clinging)	Spring	sun
North east	Chen (Stimulating)		thunder

The Pah Kwa

When these eight trigrams are placed around the compass they create a symbol called the *Pah Kwa* or the *Former Heaven Sequence*, and this octagonal arrangement is considered very lucky by the Chinese (*see* Figure 18). This pattern is found on mirrors to combat sha chi and it is also used in 'good luck' charms or talismans. A slightly different form, the Later Heaven Sequence (*see* Figure 19) is used on mariners' compasses in China. Each trigram has a certain position but the position itself changes between the two sequences. The name of each trigram is constant and what it represents (*see* table on page 75) also remains the same.

Also at the cardinal points of the compass in Feng Shui are usually depicted one of the four elements, water, fire, metal

Figure 18: The Former Heaven Sequence

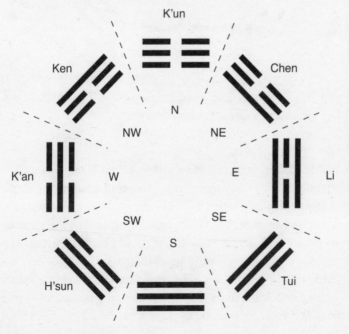

Feng Shui

Figure 19: The Later Heaven Sequence

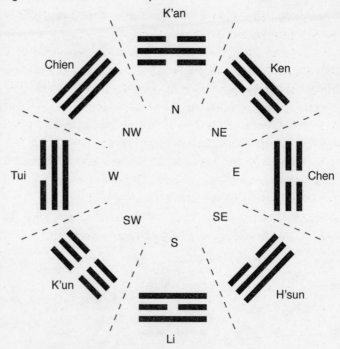

and wood. Earth is then placed in the centre. This gives us the five elements as discussed previously.

Family associations

In addition to the properties shown in the above table, each trigram is also associated with a member of a family. The core of any family, its starting point, is that of the man and woman, father and mother. You will recall that unbroken lines represent yang and among the attributes and characteristics is the male gender. Accordingly, because the Ch'ien trigram has three unbroken lines, it can be considered to be the one which is most masculine in its nature and naturally occupies the role of father. By the same token, yin is represented by the broken

74

line and among the attributes is the feminine gender. In this case, it is K'un which has three broken lines and is therefore the most feminine and thus represents mother.

This analysis can be extended to incorporate the larger family. The trigram K'an has a central unbroken line bounded by broken lines top and bottom, implying a male with thin females. This is taken to represent the middle son and the converse applies to Li where the centre line is broken, hence this is the middle daughter. The trigrams with a broken and unbroken line at the base are the eldest daughter and eldest son respectively (the H'sun and Chen trigrams). The table below summarises this sequence and also shows the element attributed to each.

Trigram	Family Member	Element
Ch'ien	Father	metal
K'un	Mother	earth
Chen	Eldest son	wood
H'sun	Eldest daughter	wood
K'an	Middle son	water
Li	Middle daughter	fire
Ken	Youngest son	earth
Tui	Youngest daughter	metal

The Magic Square

If the octagonal shape of the Pah Kwa mentioned above is drawn out until the lines impinge upon a square, the result is what is called the magic square or Lo Shu. This has its basis also in numerology, the study of numbers and their significance, where it is found that all numbers, when their individual digits are summed, can eventually be reduced to a number between 1 and 9. The use of this square in China goes back a very long way and cannot truly be traced. As can be seen from

Figure 20: Generating the Magic Square, Lo Shu, from the Pah Kwa, and the positions of the numbers

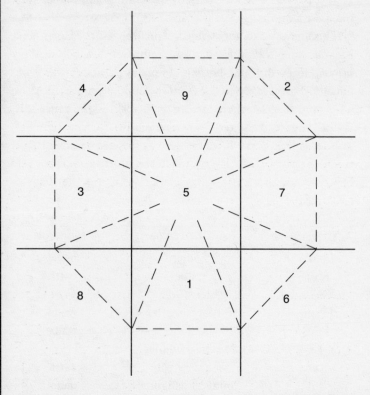

Figure 20, the numbers form a total of 15 when added across the square in any direction – horizontal, vertical or diagonal.

The Magic Square is used in many different ways by practitioners. In some cases the eight endowments are placed in the outer squares, as are animals from Chinese astrology. However, probably its main use is when initially the Feng Shui of a home or office is checked. One systematic way of doing this is to walk around the building in the order specified in the Magic Square, starting at 1 and finishing at 9 (*see* Figure 21). This is sometimes called 'Walking the Nine Palaces'.

The aim of this is to get a feel for each part of the building as your walk into it. It is only by considering the decoration, the furniture and its position, the general atmosphere of the area and what it is used for and how it is used that any improvements can be made. For example, there may be improvements in decor, type and placement of furniture and other items that could be made to improve the overall Feng Shui of the area and building. Upon finishing the process at the front door, the ideal situation would be to face south or south-east. but this will usually not be possible. However, this is not critical and there are many aspects of Feng Shui that can help improve a less than perfect situation.

Figure 21: Applying the Magic Square to checking out the Feng Shui of a building

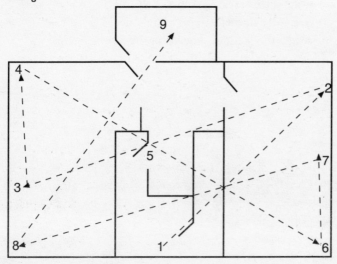

There are also matches between the facing direction of your house and the five elements, and each one of us has a certain house type that is suitable. This can be summarised as follows:

Direction of Facing	Perfect for	Reasonable for	Acceptable for	Unsuitable for
North	fire	metal	wood	water
South	water	wood	metal	fire
East	wood	fire	water	metal
West	metal	water	fire	wood

Earth types are not included because the direction has less impact upon them and they can live almost anywhere. In terms of the house types, that is, the type to match the occupants, the general guide is:

- wood – practical, unusual
- earth – family, congenial
- metal – organised, modern
- water – conservative, quiet
- fire – warm, comfortable.

(*See also* the sections on each of the five elements.)

Part II
Feng Shui:
The Practice

Feng Shui Cures

Although the essential workings of Feng Shui are relatively straightforward and can be applied logically, different practitioners develop particular ways of working. This has led to available accounts of the subject appearing quite different in many respects. We shall in this book attempt to bring together the main ways of working with Feng Shui. The interested reader will be able to grasp the fundamentals and undertake their own research, using the growing library of books now available.

By studying the various attributes of a living space its Feng Shui can be determined. Good Feng Shui can be enhanced further and bad Feng Shui can be corrected. This will apply equally to the home, garden or business premises. There are a number of techniques and actions that can be adopted and implemented to improve the Feng Shui, including the use of light, colour and linear features. Some Feng Shui consultants call these the eight remedies; here they are referred to under the general heading of 'Feng Shui Cures'. In all cases, the aim is to balance the chi, by altering, increasing or reducing it in some way.

To redress poor Feng Shui situations, attention can be paid to chi and sha chi and the counter-measures that can be employed; or the focus can be the five elements, and the need to achieve a balance. The five elements have been considered. Some indications have been given of action that can be taken to correct imbalances and conflicts and from this the general principles and practices can be determined.

When it comes to chi within the building, the primary objective is to encourage the good chi and keep out the sha chi. The chi is meant to flow around the building in a gentle fashion, unhindered by obstacles and general untidiness. The beneficial currents of chi should enter by the main door and circulate throughout the house, leaving by a window or the back entrance. On its way around the house, it should really pass through every room. When checking a house to ensure it has the optimum arrangement for the flow of chi, it should be possible to visualise a flow entering by the main door and then branching and flowing around each floor and up the stairs to the next floor. As it flows it divides to enter the various rooms with one flow continuing around the house. In this way the chi can go into each room through the door and exit either by a second door or by a window, but not by the same entrance through which it entered the room. Doors should open inwards to encourage the flow (other stipulations concerning doors are considered in the appropriate section).

Specific topics and measures are dealt with, but a few general principles can be mentioned here. It is important that the chi has the opportunity to flow around the room before leaving – if it leaves too quickly there is little opportunity for the chi to stimulate the room space. The rapid loss of chi can happen in many circumstances:

- where there are windows at opposite ends of the room
- when the stairs descend directly towards the front door
- when a house is 'divided' by a central corridor, with the back door visible from the front.

Each of these cases, and the necessary remedial action that can be taken, is described in full elsewhere.

There are many spaces in buildings that are 'dead' areas: the flow of chi is stopped, either in the corners of rooms or in rooms without windows. The corners of rooms can easily be dealt with by placing plants or ornaments in the space. Rooms that are effectively closed systems are best relegated to use as store rooms but it does help if the door opens outwards. Quite often garages (those attached to houses) are dead spaces. It will help to have a back door as well as the main entrance. However, if a bedroom is built above a garage which is a dead space there is the possibility that the bedroom will suffer from the dead chi.

Figure 22: Luo Pan, or Chinese Compass

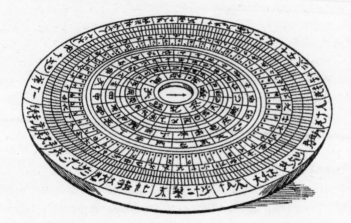

The eight remedies

When a consultant first assesses a building they may well use a Feng Shui compass, known as the Luo Pan, which consists of a board with a magnetic needle sited at the centre (Figure 22). Around this is a number of concentric circles, commonly over twenty. Contained within each ring is information that is of relevance to the Feng Shui diagnosis. The rings are set in a square-base board, thus creating a parallel with yin and yang, earth and heaven, square and circle, because the inner circular part is called the Heaven Plate and the outer square component is the Earth Plate. The compass is used by aligning it with the orientation of the building in question and information is taken from the circular parts. Further information is gleaned after matching the building with the individual's horoscope. This results in a pair of readings that usually indicate that some corrective measures are necessary. The eight categories may be used independently or together in varying amounts. They are:

- Light and mirrors
- Colour
- Linear features
- Acoustic measures
- Plants and fish
- Static elements
- Motion
- Equipment

Light and mirrors

Perhaps the commonest and most useful method of restorative action in Feng Shui, is the employment of light, mirrors and other surfaces that may reflect light in a similar way. Mirrors, in particular, are regarded as one of the most powerful tools of Feng Shui. In general, lights should be quite bright, but not too glaring as this creates an unstable environment. Outmoded fluorescent lights are inadvisable, not only because they are too bright, but because they cast eerie shadows into corners while defining sharp edges. Spotlights are best used to activate chi in negative space, such as dark corners and recesses, where the energy is likely to stagnate. Coloured lightbulbs may help to enhance one of the five elements in a room (*see* Colour page 88).

The style of a free-standing lamp or lampshade should be appropriate to the purpose for which it is being used (*see* Figure 23). Glass and metal lampshades create a more yang atmosphere while paper or fabric lanterns produce a softer, more yin effect. Crystal chandeliers are auspicious as their sparkling quality enhances sheng chi in the home – especially when used at the centre which is seen as the essence of the building. Avoid angular hi-tech or pointed designs altogether as they can cause sharp cutting chi similar to that found outside the home.

Figure 23

Bright lights should be left switched on at the entrance to homes where the area is dark and cramped. Up-lighters, which are helpful in correcting the effects of a low or sloping ceiling, create a more subdued yin effect. In China, light is often used in the garden and around the outside walls of a house. Spotlights are sometimes used as a corrective measure to square off an L-shaped house, in effect creating two extra 'walls'.

Feng Shui consultants often use concave mirrors to *neutralise* the effect of a negative image and convex mirrors to *minimise* the effect of a negative image, but for use around the home a plain mirror should be sufficient. Mirrors help to illuminate dark rooms and are especially useful for corners that, without a direct source of light, would remain dark. They enable bad chi to be directed back out of a building or, by locating them in particular positions, good chi can be brought in – by enlightening a particular aspect of the room, or by reflecting a pleasant view from outside, perhaps a snapshot of the garden or a body of water.

Chi can be directed into corners and, by the prudent use of light and mirrors, a room can be improved immeasurably. Mirrors also encourage the flow of chi around the room and are therefore positioned in the dead spaces or where the flow of chi would otherwise stop. All objects which have a reflective quality, such as tapestries with sequins and shiny discs activate chi. However, mirror tiles – which distort whatever they reflect – are inadvisable. It goes without saying that cracked mirrors should never be used in the home.

It should also be remembered that too many mirrors can be a bad thing in certain rooms, such as the bedroom where a restful atmosphere is needed. Here mirrors can energise the chi too much, causing sleepless nights. A lounge should not have too many mirrors either. The incorrect placement of mirrors may upset the harmony of your home. and there are certain locations where you should avoid them altogether. For example, you should avoid placing a mirror on the ceiling, especially above the bed, where it can suggest illness and immobility, or above the dining table, where the sight of yourself upside down can cause distress and digestive problems.

Other areas where you should not place a mirror are: facing the front door; reflecting a door or a bed; on the rear wall or tiger wall of a room; reflecting clutter or rubbish; or behind an office chair. In an office, mirrors should not reflect the exit or coffee machine as this will reduce concentration. Mirrors should not 'bring' any negative landscapes or features into the home – be mindful as to what is outside when placing them near or opposite windows.

Colour

Many people tend to decorate their house with relatively quiet shades and perhaps only the younger generations opt for strong, loud colour schemes. However, colours can be used to help the flow of chi and a bright area in an otherwise dull room can help enormously. The Chinese certainly follow this practice and commonly use red and black as these are deemed particularly fortuitous when it comes to financial matters. Of course, the significance of a particular colour can vary from culture to culture, and you may want to use your discretion when decorating your home — after all, you have to be able to live with your walls! Nevertheless, it is worth understanding the symbolic value of the colours in Feng Shui, as outlined below. (For application on a room-by-room basis, see the relevant sections in Inside Your Home, page 111.)

Black symbolises water and rules the north. If overused, this colour's yin energy can have a depressing effect, but too little can sap your energy and cause feelings of uncertainty. It is best used to frame other colours.

Blue also symbolises water, and rules the north-east and the south-east. Too much blue in your house will lead to indecision but, like black, the right amount can create clarity and precision.

Green is the colour of wood and signifies growth. As the moderator between water and fire, green represents movement and possibility. Again, too much of this colour can be counter-productive and may lead to naive idealism. To balance your home with green, it may be sufficient to have well-placed leafy plants.

Yellow is the colour of earth, and associated with both intellect and society, creating strong social energy. It is one of the most important colours in China, but too much of it may lead the occupant to suffer from delusions of grandeur.

Red represents fire, and is the most stimulating colour in the spectrum. It encourages activity but, when used to excess, can contribute to excitement, anxiety, tension headaches and even violence. Avoid using this colour in a nursery or bedroom. However, it may help combat listlessness and when combined with yellow produces a very dynamic energy – seen in action in many fast food chains.

White represents metal, yang and purity. It reflects light and is often seen in Feng Shui as a weak mirror which might be used to offset minor Feng Shui problems, such as irregular room shapes or lack of natural light.

Orange is a mixture of fire and earth, and may be good for offsetting too much of the water element. It is also associated with socialising and would be more suited to the lounge than the bedroom or quiet areas of the home.

Violet is a combination of fire and water, and is a great colour to use in a room which is already well-balanced. This colour is unsuitable for a home office or business as it can cause drowsiness, and is best used in a quiet area. Too much violet may lead you to isolate yourself from others.

Brown is the colour of earth, but for interior decoration it causes an excess of yin energy and is to be avoided. Light brown is especially unfavourable because in China it was traditionally associated with death. As a symbol of the wood element, the use of wood for floors and furniture has slightly different application (*see* Interior Decoration/Texture, page 182).

Grey is a combination of black and white, and thus neutral. Central to the philosophy of Feng Shui is the unity of opposites, yin and yang, and as grey represents neither, it is not highly regarded for interior decoration. It is also excessively yin.

Gold is an element of metal and a symbol of wealth. In slight touches, such as gilt picture frames or brass handles, it cannot fail to have a positive effect on the fortunes of a household.

Silver is a symbol of metal associated with the moon, which has both positive and negative properties. As a metal it is also a symbol of wealth.

Pastels, with the exception of light brown, can be seen as a diluted form of the colour closest to them. Off-white, for example, dilutes the dazzling mirror effect of white, but pastels may be too weak when a certain colour is needed to remedy an unfavourable Feng Shui situation.

Linear features

When it becomes necessary to divert the flow of chi, as often happens when it moves too quickly (in long corridors, for example), linear features can be very useful. The feature may be a fan, sword, bamboo tube or one of a number of items that are placed at an angle (across the corridor) to redirect the chi back into rooms (Figure 24). However, you should not place a sword directly opposite the front door as this can 'cut' the chi entering your home. Sword shapes should not be placed in children's rooms.

Figure 24

Acoustic measures

Noise, particularly if it is melodic and harmonious, can break up chi that has become sluggish because it generates sound waves in the air. In addition to moving chi, musical noises are also said to foster wealth by attracting lucky chi into a building. Many people like wind chimes and without appreciating how they can help, suspend them in their porch or kitchen. Wind chimes, bells, and mobiles that create some sort of musical tinkling are all useful in this respect. However, for the purposes of restorative action the wind chimes should usually be made of metal. They will be less effectual if made from glass, shells or wood, or if brightly coloured. Where a wind chime is hung in a place with no breeze, it should be struck from time to time. A silent wind chime will do little to improve the Feng Shui of your home!

Plants and fish

Living things in general can be very useful to move or slow down chi, and this includes plants and also, for example, fish. Plants can be placed in areas where there is no chi, and in locations where the chi needs to be stirred up, as well as softening corners which might produce arrows of chi. Large plants will slow down chi when it is moving too quickly. Broad-leafed plants, such as the money plant, are particularly auspicious (Figure 25). Bonsai trees and cacti with prickles are not. In particular, avoid placing spiky plants such as cacti or yuccas in the bedroom or near any chair in the house as they can direct arrows of chi at the seated or sleeping person.

Figure 25: A money plant

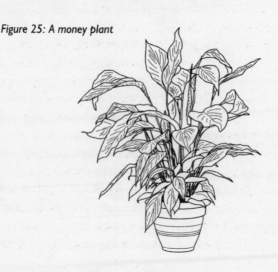

An unpleasant view can be blocked by a window box, enhancing the flow of positive chi in the room at the same time. Bushy plants should be placed in front of protruding corners to soften the effects of cutting chi, while staggering them either side of a straight, narrow corridor helps to slow fast-moving sha chi. Plants with slightly more pointed leaves are suitable for dark corners where chi is likely to stagnate. In moderation, plants can be placed in the kitchen and bedroom, and are particularly good for helping the movement of chi in the bathroom. Hanging plants should not be placed in the main bedroom, however, nor should too many plants be placed at the centre of the house. Many Feng Shui practitioners believe dried flowers should not be brought into the home, although not all are agreed on this. At any rate, a dead plant or flower will certainly not act as a Feng Shui cure!

Fish in an aquarium can be useful to promote the favourable flow of chi, in addition to providing an interesting and sometimes almost hypnotic focus. An aquarium is often regarded as a 'double' Feng Shui cure since bubbling water and fish both activate chi. New homeowners in Hong Kong sometimes install a fish tank containing several blackmoles, or blackmoors, and one goldfish near the door. Fish are believed to absorb negative chi left behind by the previous owner of inherent in the house and the blackmole variety is particularly sensitive. When they die – a sign that there is much negative energy – they are replaced, and this process continues until all of the negative chi has been absorbed.

There are many rules regarding aquariums which most Feng Shui practitioners will observe. The colour of the fish is one of these. Black, gold and silver fish are ideal, but there should not be too many red fish as this colour belongs to the fire element, which conflicts with water. Brightly coloured and quick darting fish will create a more active yang energy while slow, darker coloured fish are more yin, promoting a more relaxing environment. To enhance financial prosperity, there should be one, six, eight or nine fish. A tank containing two, five, seven or ten fish is bad – so if your eighth fish dies, replacing it is a matter of some urgency. The aquarium should be round, cylindrical, hexagonal or rectangular, but square and triangular tanks, which represent earth and fire respectively, are at odds with the water element. Natural materials such as pebbles, shells and living plants should be used instead of plastic, and decorations should be simple. The aquarium can be located in the east or south east of the house, ideally in the lounge.

Static elements

This generally applies to features outside where it may become necessary to decelerate the flow of chi. This may be the case in a garden, where any large object, such as a rock or statue, will help to compensate for fast-moving chi. If a statue is used, it should blend in with the surroundings and with the personality of the individual. Heavy furniture can be used indoors for the same purpose, and may be a source of support when during times of uncertainty and instability. However, there are other things that need to be taken into account when using furniture as a Feng Shui cure (*see*, for example, Interior Decoration/Household accessories/Antiques, page 191).

Motion

The movement of an object can help divert or animate chi and the Chinese commonly use items such as flags, ribbons, chimes and mobiles, and fountains (Figure 26). Ideally the wind should be the motivating force. Flowing water is helpful in bringing in chi, but it should not flow too rapidly.

Figure 26

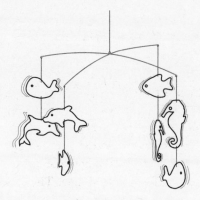

Equipment

This includes all types of machine and items of electrical equipment which can vitalise chi, but it is necessary to ensure that it is not overdone. A balance has to be achieved between the electricity which is used in so many modern appliances, from fridges to microwaves to computers, and the chi. The best approach to adopt is to keep such usage to a sensible minimum. This is particularly important in the bedroom, where chi need not be too active. Washing machines and refrigerators are balanced by the yin chi of water, but special rules involving the placement of these items are considered in later sections (*see* Inside Your Home/The Kitchen, page 143).

In later sections, the way in which these actions can be applied to Feng Shui are described in more detail. There are numerous examples of such applications throughout the book, particularly when a moderating element is required. However, before you can begin applying the cures, you need to have some understanding of how to evaluate the existing Feng Shui of your building.

Assessing
Your Building

Feng Shui practitioners believe that environmental factors, i.e. the places where you live and work, have a profound influence on all areas of your life and the events that take place around you. A run of bad luck, a series of accidents, a catalogue of romantic failures or a bout of ill health are all part of a negative energy field which can often be traced back to your surroundings. Therefore, any spell of bad fortune should give you cause to examine your home and work environment. If you are planning to move house or make alterations to your current home, it is worth consulting the relevant sections in this book before you begin, to ensure that any changes you make are for the better. This section looks at some of the methods for assessing your building.

Symbolic animals

In addition to all the other factors involved in Feng Shui, there are aspects of astrology and astronomy involved. Four terms derived from Chinese astronomy are used in Feng Shui, being placed at the points of the compass. These four animals, the tortoise (or turtle), the phoenix (or bird), the dragon and the tiger are also associated with directions as applied to a house, and with the seasons. Each animal (often called a celestial animal) has particular associations in terms of character and emotions. These are shown in greater detail in the table shown opposite.

These animal symbols are used to assess the Feng Shui of a house with respect to its position. When a house faces south, into the realm of the red phoenix, then the terms front, back, etc. coincide with the compass directions, i.e. looking out of the house to the south means you are also facing away from the front.

Leaving your house to go into the realm of the red bird is

Figure 27

back door

front door

supposed to bring good luck and good fortune. In China it is common practice for people to seek a house that is either south or south-east facing. This is an auspicious set-up as it allows into the house the good fortune of the bird (for south facing) and in addition the wisdom of the dragon (for south-east facing). In front of the house, the ground should gently fall away (*see* Figure 27 *and* Inside Your Home/Doors, apge 113). If the drop is too steep then it is believed the red bird will 'fall off', thus adversely affecting your fortune.

With this configuration in mind, the back of the house would be the area of the black tortoise or turtle. This is the area of mystery, but can perhaps be more logically interpreted as the realm of private matters, including marriage and family concerns. Referring again to Figure 27, the hills behind the house are necessary to provide protection and keep close at hand all that is of importance at this personal level.

To the east ideally there should be hills of the green dragon representing good luck and also hope. To the west is the realm of the white tiger. The land to the west should be flat (*see* Figure 28). Anything else may generate bad luck – hills will mean that the white tiger will be strong with an abundance of the characteristics listed above. This could lead to difficulties in your personal life. If the ground to the west rapidly slopes

Figure 28: The symbolic animals in relation to the home

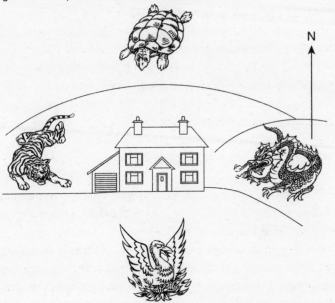

away, then the tiger's influence will be minimal and this can lead to an existence without interest or any excitement. This is the ideal situation but, since this is out of reach for most of us, the Feng Shui of our home interior is important in counteracting any negative aspects outside. This is dealt with later in the book.

The symbolic animals are also used with reference to the walls of the house and the directions in which they face. In a house facing south, the entrance wall is attributed to the bird (compass direction south) but the interior wall facing the entrance is also designated by the bird. However, the outside of that same wall is in the realm of the tortoise because it faces north. By the same token, the other walls can be attributed to the other animals, each being allocated one internal and one external wall dependent upon the direction of facing.

Thus, from this perspective, the best configuration for a house is where the four symbolic animals can be discerned in the outlines of the scenery round about the site. The dragon is regarded as the most important and at the very least it is hoped that a hill to the east can be taken to represent the green dragon. When one of the four animals can be identified in the scenery, then the directions of the other three can obviously be established, even if there are no physical signs of them.

Methods used in Feng Shui

When an individual appraises their home using Feng Shui or when a consultant is called in to a home or office, there are several methods that can be used to sort out the problems. In all cases the result is that the layout of the room will almost certainly be altered and additional items will be installed, as summarised in the preceding chapter. One method of analysis commonly used is based upon the octagonal structure of the Pah Kwa (*see* page 73). There are two techniques based upon this basic configuration, one called the eight-point method and the other, the eight enrichments or endowment method.

Figure 29: The areas of the eight enrichments or endowments

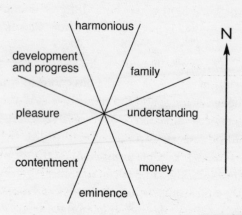

The latter consists of laying over the plan of the house in question the octagonal grid (*see* Figure 29) and this enables the problem areas to be determined and improvements to be suggested (for convenience this has been shown with the north area to the top). The eight point method involves placing a star made up of eight lines (*see* Figure 30, page 104) over the plan of the house or individual rooms to see where the lines impinge upon the walls. Both techniques will be described briefly and their application will then be encountered later in this book.

The endowment method

This derives its name from the aspect of a person's house. The direction in which it faces enriches the house in a particular way, thus north represents harmonious relationships and east understanding, as listed:

Facing Direction	Endowment
north	harmonious relationships
north east	family
east	understanding
south east	money
south	eminence
south west	contentment
west	pleasure
north west	developments and progress

By studying a house plan with reference to the grid, it is possible to determine which rooms/areas fall under which particular influence and how best this combination can be altered or improved. The grid should always be placed facing south even if the main door to the house does not. The position of the door and its direction of facing is quite important and will be considered in a later section.

The eight-point method

This method is used by many practitioners of Feng Shui, and is covered extensively by Simons (in *Feng Shui Step by Step*, 1996). In this case the eight-fold grid comprises eight points or areas covering such aspects as finance, eminence (or reputation), wisdom (or knowledge), career and so on (*see* Figure 30). Once again the grid is placed over the ground plan of the house in question and the wall that contains the main door should also contain the points for wisdom, career and friends (or 8, 1 and 6 in Figure 21, page 77).

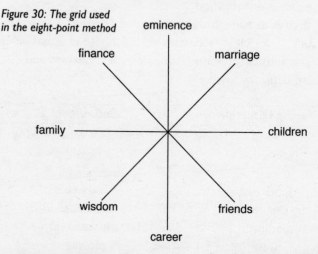

Figure 30: The grid used
in the eight-point method

eminence

finance   marriage

family ——————— children

wisdom   friends

career

The grid can also be placed over individual rooms and this is often necessary if a house has an unusual ground plan. The placing of the eight points is achieved by standing at the door and imagining that you are looking in, thus eminence is furthest away and finance is away in the left-hand corner (Figure 31). Where the outline of a room does not readily fit with the regular arrangement of points, and many rooms will fall into this category, there are a number of procedures suggested to obtain the best possible placing of points:

Figure 31: Superimposing the eight points on a room plan

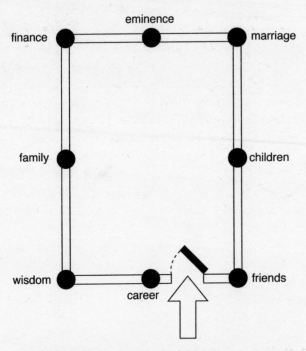

- The boundary of the room can be projected until a more regular shape is created (Figure 32) upon which the points can be placed. However this does not necessarily clarify the placing of points.
- Where spaces, say in two adjoining rooms, clearly do not accommodate the eight points, it is better to treat them as separate rooms, applying the same principles and standing in each doorway, looking in, to place the points (Figure 33). In this case there is no place for finance and wisdom because they are outside the room boundary. However, if the smaller extension is treated as a separate room then all the points can be applied quite easily (Figure 34).

Figure 32

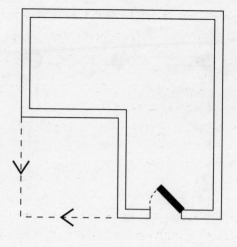

Figure 33

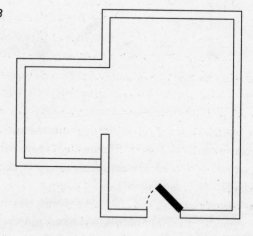

- Other rooms may have an irregular shape, which presents you with more than one option for placing the eight points. In this case the points can either be placed to include as much of the space of the room as possible or the room can be divided as described above, to create more manageable shapes. If necessary, walls can temporarily be created by the use of partitions thus enabling the points to be placed.

Figure 34: Application of the eight-point method to a room extension

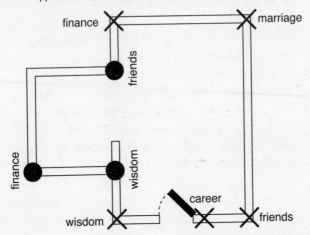

The eight point method and the endowment method are just two of the ways in which the Feng Shui of a building can be analysed. They are also among the easiest. With some relatively straightforward preparation, you can use one of these methods as the starting point for practising Feng Shui in your own home.

Preparation and tools

The three vital tools for preparing your own Feng Shui analysis are the Pah Kwa, the floor plan and the compass. Making sure your Pah Kwa is accurate, your floor plan is to scale, and that you have invested in a good quality compass are all worth the effort. Any inaccuracies at this stage could lead to mistakenly applied cures, leaving your home with less favourable conditions than before you began.

CHECKLIST I Preparation/tools

You will need:

- graph paper for an accurate floor plan
- cardboard to stick to the graph paper if your house is an irregular shape
- a skewer for finding the centre of an irregular-shaped home
- tracing paper for your Pah Kwa
- a compass for finding the directions of your home
- a 360-degree protractor for drawing your Pah Kwa
- a pair of compasses for drawing your Pah Kwa
- a ruler for drawing your floor plan to scale
- a measuring tape for the measurements of your home
- a sharp pencil.

If you have recently bought a new home, you may have been given an accurate floor plan with your documents. However, it is worth double-checking the measurements of all interior and exterior walls, including alcoves, staircases, doors, windows, and fitments. Locate the areas where you intend to place movable furniture such as beds, desks and electrical equipment. You should record whether the doors open into or out of the room, and highlight any Feng Shui 'problem areas', such as protrusions or sloping ceilings.

Use a scale that is appropriate to the size of your house – 1cm for every metre will be easy to convert and suitable for the size of many homes. After measuring the size of your house, measure the size of each room. You will have one floor plan for every floor in your house. Drawing the plan on graph paper will help with the measurements but, for reasons outlined below, unless your house is a perfect square or rectangle, you should stick the paper to a piece of cardboard and cut them to the shape of the floor plan.

Finding the centre of a square or rectangular house is simple indeed – just draw two diagonal lines from corner to corner on the plan. If your house has an irregular shape, one quick and fairly accurate method is to balance the floor plan (cut to the shape of the house in cardboard) on a cooking skewer. The point at which the cardboard balances is the centre. (However, in an L-shaped house the centre will probably be outside.) Finding the direction of your home should be less of a problem, using your compass, but don't accept the first reading – walk around your home until you get the precise bearings, and record them.

The next stage is to design the Pah Kwa. This is best drawn on tracing paper or other transparent material, using a pair of compasses and a protractor. Mark the centre, and the north point with a dotted line, and divide into eight even sections. If you are using the endowment method, each section corresponds to a direction (*see* Figure 29) – north (harmony), north east (family), east (understanding), south east (money), south (eminence), south west (contentment), west (pleasure) and north west (development and progress). Cut this out.

When you are satisfied with both your floor plan and your Pah Kwa, place the plan on a flat surface with the walls of the plan aligned to the same walls of the house. Place the centre of the compass over the centre of the plan and turn until the compass needle is aligned with the marker line, then mark this point, drawing a line to the centre. Hold the Pah Kwa over the floor plan, turning until the centres and the north-pointing lines are aligned. The same method can be used to assess each of the main rooms.

Remember that if you are using the eight-point method, the analysis of your house plan will be slightly different. The main entrance should be at the bottom of the page facing down, and the wall containing the main door should contain the points for wisdom, career and friends (*see* page 107 and Figure 34.

Also see Inside Your Home/Doors for what constitutes the main entrance).

When you have placed the Pah Kwa over the finished floor plan, you can begin to identify the characteristics of each section of the house and any problem areas resulting from the location of those characteristics. If you have just moved or are renovating a house, you may well be in a position to allocate rooms according to the most favourable positions indicated by the grid. If this is not possible, you will at least be able to pinpoint the areas that need attention.

The following sections look at a variety of topics from doors and windows to gardens, pointing out what can be done to make your overall environment a more harmonious one in which to live.

Inside Your Home

The door is the portal, the focus of any building whether a home or an office. Since this is the point where chi enters and is distributed through the building, it is vital to the well-being of the occupants that the front door is located favourably on the house plan and in relation to the outside environment. This then is an appropriate place to start.

Doors

External doors

Perhaps the most important door is the front door and although it may not be feasible to relocate it to a more beneficial position, it is possible to lessen any deficits. First of all, you need to ascertain which door is your front door. That may seem obvious, but for many people the back door is the main entry and exit point. However much it may look like the front door, if the main entrance is blocked off by furniture or boxes it is not the point at which chi enters your home. Additionally, if your front door is never used by you or your visitors, and has not been used for years, then your back door is your main entrance for the purposes of placing the Pah Kwa and assessing the influence of the symbolic animals (*see* Figure 28). But if you and your visitors rarely use the front door but do so on occasion, this remains your front door. When in doubt, use the door that architecturally resembles the main entrance, but don't assume it is the entry point for chi just because it looks as if it should be!

A door that is too large may allow a lot of chi to escape while a door that is too small may need to appear to be larger. To prevent chi escaping, wind chimes, a banner or something similar can be hung by the door to slow down the chi and direct it back into the building. The front door should be larger than the back door to prevent chi leaving the house too quickly and both doors should be proportional to the size of the house. A doorway can easily be made to appear larger by the careful placing of mirrors. This will also help by reflecting pleasant outside views into the entrance hall (assuming there is a pleasant view to be reflected), porch or room and it should facilitate the escape of bad chi and may enlighten a darker corner in the entrance area, perhaps an area in shadow behind the door. It is unfavourable for the door to be reached by means of a narrow passageway or for it to be enclosed on three sides.

Even the design of the door has some relevance in Feng Shui. It is considered unlucky if the main door has too elaborate a design and, if it is made up of panels, they should be of equal dimensions. Sturdy doors which are simple and elegant are most desirable – a semi-circular doorway or a semi-circular window above the door is particularly auspicious, as are symmetrical double doors. In an office building, a revolving circular door encourages positive chi to enter. It almost goes without saying that the doorway should not have too many angles, as these can direct 'secret arrows' into your home .

A fully- or semi-glazed front or back door allows both light and chi into the home in a favourable position. This is especially helpful if the porch or hallway is dark and cramped, as the chi may otherwise stagnate. However, it is important that the main door looks like a main door. Hinges and locks should be well-oiled and paintwork should not be permitted to flake or fade, nor should dustbins or refuse be placed outside the entrance. The door should be aligned with the main wall and not located in a protrusion or hollow in the house. It is unfavourable for the front of the house to have two or more doors or gates, as this can cause conflict between occupants. In general, too many openings to the house also result in the benefits of chi being dissipated. This applies to windows, French windows, rear and side doors, skylights and atriums.

Conversely, a house with too little natural light and ventilation allows the chi to stagnate, causing health problems.

The direction in which the door faces is also important and, as already mentioned, the most auspicious position is south facing. Front doors facing east and south east are also favourable positions, the former ideal for young people at the start of a career or marriage, the latter representing communication and harmony. To make the most of a beneficial location for the front of the house, the main door should face in the same direction. Using a glazed or partially glazed door here will allow more positive chi into the home.

There are many measures that can be taken to improve a less propitious direction of facing, such as north which can be too isolating. Painting the front door a bright colour, especially red, may stimulate chi in the north. An outside light here would also be helpful. The sharp fast-moving chi of the north east can be deflected away from the house by a glossy white door with brass fittings, as shiny metals act in much the same way as mirrors. This would also be useful to deflect cutting chi from a sharp corner or post outside the house. When the location of the front of the house and the direction of the front door are different, the location will have the more influence, but a door facing a different direction can, to some extent, help to balance an unfavourable location. A smaller door will be appropriate when the direction is a negative one.

The door is important in many other respects, not least in the view gained on leaving the building and the impression created on entering. It is preferable not to have the door facing objects that are effectively blocking the view; for example, a tree, lamp post, telegraph pole, the corner of another building or a hill. Sharp objects pointed towards the door also generate harmful sha chi (*see* Figures 5 and 6). The general rule is if it is within a 45-degree range of your front door the object needs to be addressed by using one of the eight Feng Shui remedies. In most cases it is not possible to resolve the situation by removing the obstacle, but this may be feasible with large bushes or small trees which can interfere with the chi. It may, in any case, be advisable to have a tree removed that is very close to your house as the roots could easily disrupt the foundations of the building, particularly in dry weather, although it is not good Feng Shui to chop down a mature tree (*see* Designing Your Garden, page 223).

The removal of an obstacle to chi will improve your wealth, but if the obstacle cannot be removed, it should be balanced by the careful positioning of other items such as potted plants, statues or similar items. A tree directly in front of your door becomes a help instead of a hindrance when there is a more negative object behind it, such as an electricity pylon or chimney stack. In Hong Kong, the primordial Pah Kwa is often placed over the front door as a matter of course, but can also

Figure 35: Balancing obstacles

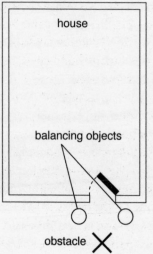
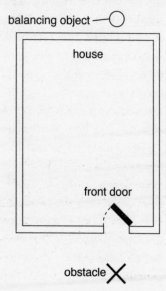

Figure 36: A gentle slope falling from the front door [good Feng Shui]

protect the home from harmful arrows of chi (*see* Figure 1, page 14). An alternative is to place an object behind the house, positioned such that it mirrors the obstacle at the front (*see* Figure 35) thus balancing the negative effect.

Other unfavourable positions for the main door are opposite a neighbour's gate, main door or driveway, and facing a T-junction, a church or a police station. These are considered in detail in later sections (*see* Outside Your Home/The immediate surroundings). While it is preferable for the door to open onto land that is flat or that slopes away gently (Figure 36), it is relatively easy to counteract any negative features in the surrounding ground. Rising ground in front of the house is unfavourable because a situation where it is necessary to go up a hill to leave a house reflects problems in your day to day life – each day becomes a struggle. The reverse situation, where chi is encouraged to exit the house too quickly by steep ground running away from the house, is also negative. Both situations may be remedied by a row of small trees in front of the house (Figure 37).

Figure 37: A steep hill modified by a row of trees [modified Feng Shui]

Steps outside the front door have much the same effect as hills, hastening or easing the flow of chi in and out of the home. It is better to have steps rising to the house than descending because in basement flats, for example, chi can stagnate outside the front door. While bushes and shrubs outside the home will slow the chi flowing away from your home, tall plants can help sheng chi flow up the steps and into your front door.

A very negative position is when a house is situated on a hill or slope with the front door positioned above the back door. This is very detrimental because it allows sha chi to enter the house and it also can lead to a loss of wealth and well-being. However, there is a very simple and favourable solution that has been adopted in many cases, and this is to reverse the doors and use the back door as the main door and vice versa. This creates ideal Feng Shui and this configuration is sometimes called 'sitting on solid ground viewing the sky.' There are also changes that can be made in the approaches to a house that will improve its Feng Shui – for example modifying the

Figure 38

paths – and these will be considered in a later section (*see* Designing your Garden, page 221).

When opening the main door into the house, it should ideally be hinged at the side of the nearest wall so that the door opens towards that wall (Figure 38). This conveys a feeling of space and welcome and it readily lends itself to good Feng Shui. The opposite, where the door opens towards the space of the room immediately restricts whoever is entering. When the door is open, it is important that the chi is not allowed to flow straight through the house and out of the back door or a window. This will indeed be the case if on entering it is possible to see the back door , providing a rapid route for the chi to exit (Figure 39). To avoid this happening, barriers must be placed in the path of the chi and this can be done with mirrors, screens, plants on a unit, or something similar and if there is a window, then a curtain or blinds will act to stop the draining of chi. If, as in Figure 39, it is difficult to place a physical barrier between the front and back doors, then a curtain on the door itself would help to some extent. The curtain need not be a heavy velvet material; a fine lace curtain would both look attractive and serve the purpose. It would also allow light to enter if the door was glazed or partially glazed.

When entering a building, be it home or office, it is prefer-

Figure 39

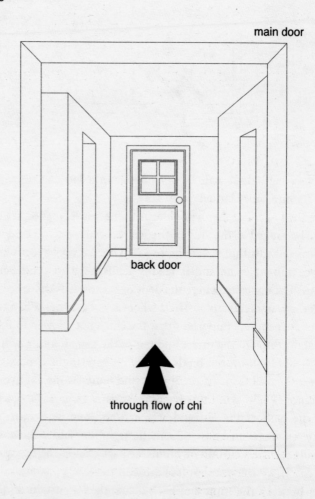

main door

back door

through flow of chi

able to be faced with a balanced interior. If this is not the case – if, for example, on entering you immediately face the corner of a wall or the edge of a large cupboard this can be counterbalanced by the use of a mirror, screen or a plant or decorative ornament (*see* Figure 40).

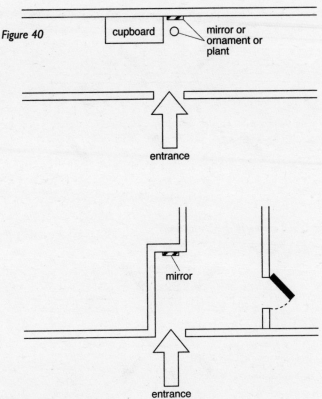

Figure 40

CHECKLIST 2 Inside your home/doors

Your home will suffer if the main entrance:

- faces a staircase
- faces a corner
- faces a column or post
- is visible from the back door
- has a view of a washbasin or toilet
- has a view of a stove or fireplace
- faces the door of a bedroom
- faces the door of a sitting room
- is situated below a toilet.

121

Figure 41a: An ideal arrangement of doors

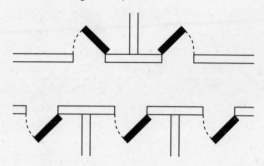

Figure 41b: A good arrangement of doors

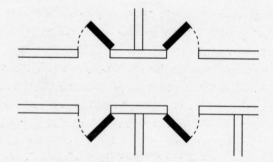

Figure 41c: A poor arrangement of doors

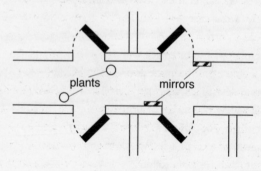

plants

mirrors

Internal doors

When starting from scratch, that is, when designing a new house or undertaking major alterations, all aspects of Feng Shui can be accounted for and the juxtaposition of doors, walls and so on can be placed to their greatest benefit. Many buildings, particularly offices, have quite long corridors containing a number of doors into rooms. Too many doors in a corridor or hallway can lead to confusion and ideally doors should be placed at regular intervals. Some advocate doors facing each other while others regard this as a potential source of disharmony and in any event too public an arrangement.

Doors should certainly not overlap each other a little as this indicates antagonism and probably the best arrangement, if a number of doors are necessary, is to have them regularly spaced (*see* Figures 41a and 41b). Where this ideal arrangement is not possible, the remedy is to use mirrors opposite the doors which conflict, or possibly strategically placed attractive plants (*see* Figure 41c). In addition, the immediate area can be improved through the use of suitable lighting and internal decor. A room situated at the end of a hallway or corridor, particularly if the corridor is long, is likely to suffer from sha chi and this can be corrected by fastening a long mirror to the side of the door facing the corridor. Another situation that creates conflict is when three doors face each other from three different directions. In this case, a wind chime should be hung from the ceiling between the three doors.

It hardly needs stating because it is so obvious, but doors should be easy to open and should not be hindered in their opening by furniture inside the room. Leaving doors open will encourage the free flow of chi, but in the bathroom the door should be kept shut. It is not always possible to arrange the furniture in a room precisely as required, but every effort should be made to provide easy access into the room. Later sections will concentrate upon how furniture can best be placed in rooms.

Windows

In many respects, windows should be considered in much the same light as doors, and some mention has already been made of preventing chi flowing in at the main door and straight out of the back door or a window. The arrangement of a room and the articles within it should be so as to promote the smooth flow of chi entering and leaving the room. To prevent the rapid loss of chi, should this be happening, we can to some extent refer to the remedies suggested already – such as covering the window with a curtain, even if the curtain is made only of lace.

Cross-ventilation, where two windows are directly opposite one another, means a room cannot hold chi, and this can lead to a corresponding loss of money and health. Too many windows, or openings that are too large, meanwhile, result in the benefits of chi being dissipated. It is also believed that too many windows will lead to family conflict. A room with more than two walls of windows has too much ventilation, and this can lead to excessive yang energy if the window is on the sunny side of the house. Here stained glass or small panes would help slow down the flow of chi. Crystals or wind chimes would also be useful in this case.

Obviously, a room with no or very small windows will suffer from too little ventilation. Houses in which all the windows face north could suffer from this problem, as well as L-shaped houses where part of the house might be in shade for most of the day. The skilful use of lighting, especially candles, and natural wood surfaces and plants will help readjust the north and north east sectors of your home. Windows facing east will bring the chi energy of sunrise into the home, pro-

124

moting energy and positive thinking. Windows facing west bring the chi energy of sunset into the home, helping you to relax and wind down. If you have a house with both east and west facing windows, consider allocating the rooms you use for evening relaxation to the west and daytime activities to the east.

A general principle is that windows (and doors) should not be sited near to the corner of a room as this enables the chi to move out of the room too quickly. If the eight points (mentioned earlier) are superimposed on the room, it will be seen in which category there will be a loss of chi and therefore a negative effect on one aspect of your life. If, for example the chi flows quickly through and out of the room as shown in Figure 42 at the point where the area for children is situated, then one may expect some difficulties in that aspect of your personal life. This room clearly also has some negative features with

Figure 42

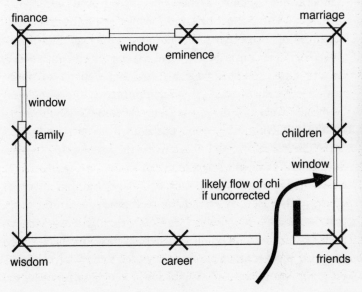

regard to the friends aspect and the confining nature of the door. This will need some remedial action as it is better not to have doors or windows at the corners of rooms – in this case there is a danger of losing chi too rapidly in the area of friends. To counteract the rapid exit of chi through the side window, a simple lace curtain and perhaps a small vase of flowers would provide the ideal solution. A relatively simple action can have a proportionately far greater positive effect.

As with doors, some window shapes are more favourable than others for different areas of the house. A square or wide rectangular shaped window represents the earth element and promotes stability, while a round window represents the metal element and promotes focus and determination. A tall, narrow window represents tree energy, promoting communication and harmony. Whatever the shape or size of the window, it is inadvisable to place a bed or a stove beneath it, or to relax or study with your back to the window. It is probably the standard, but windows are best opening outwards and opening fully. This, it is believed, brings good fortune and enhanced opportunities to the occupants. In Feng Shui windows that open inwards will have adverse effects on health, finance and career. If your windows do happen to open inwards, it is also a good idea to determine what sort of chi is being admitted (*see* Assessing Your Building/Symbolic animals *and* Outside Your Home/The immediate surroundings). If the chi is negative and disruptive – that is, sha chi – it can be diverted or blocked by the use of a vase of flowers at the window, hanging wind chimes or something similar, or a strategically placed mirror if the configuration of the room permits this. Many windows do not open completely, either because they are sash windows where at most one half of the aperture is covered, or because they are modern UPVC double glazed units that have a fixed lower panel and an opening upper panel. In these cases it will help to place flowers at the lower closed part of the window.

The type of window treatment you choose may help to redress an imbalance of chi or it may make matters worse. Curtains inhibit the flow of chi, especially if they are made of heavy fabric, and this may be needed where a view is unfavourable or in the bedroom where the bed is near the window. In small rooms or at small windows, curtains could inhibit the flow of chi to such an extent that it stagnates. Windows that have unfavourable views are best fitted with venetian blinds, with the slats adjusted so that they block the view without obstructing natural light. A window box just outside the window will also be helpful. In extreme cases, a Feng Shui consultant might advise a client to block up a window altogether – though this is rarely practicable. Shutters might serve the purpose for an extremely offensive view. Conversely, you can make the most of a beautiful view by placing a mirror at right angles to the window – provided the mirror does not reflect a main door as well. For the effects of different materials on the flow of chi, see Interior Decoration/Texture.

CHECKLIST 3 Doors/ windows

- A main door that is too small can be remedied by the careful use of mirrors.
- A wind chime may be placed by a main door which is too large to prevent chi escaping.
- The main door should be hinged at the side of the nearest wall.
- Furniture should not hinder the easy opening of doors
- If the back door or window can be seen from the front, obstacles such as mirrors, screens, plants and curtains must be used to prevent chi flowing straight in one way and out of the other.

- Too many doors in a corridor can lead to confusion.
- Doors and windows should not be sited near the corner of the room or chi will be lost too rapidly.
- When windows do not open completely, it is helpful to place flowers at the closed section.
- A room situated at the end of a hallway is likely to suffer from sha chi, which can be corrected by placing a long mirror to the side of this door.

The entrance hall

There are many houses where entry is made directly from the street into a room. However, most buildings have an entrance hall of some description albeit rather small, and there is a tremendous variety in the nature of the entrance hall and the available space. Homes with a small room of this nature will clearly be a little more private and can be quieter than arrangements where there is no hall.

General principles are that a window in the hall is useful to ensure that the chi moves around – it is not good for the chi to become too static. It is not ideal to have the front door opening onto a small hall from which a staircase ascends, as it is very likely that the chi in this situation will flow straight out of the door. It then becomes necessary to slow down the chi to prevent this happening and this can be accomplished by hanging wind chimes (*see* Figure 43). It is not possible to use a mirror in this situation, but a plant set on a stand could help matters. If the stairs are at an angle to the outside door, then a mirror can be used to divert the chi and also to provide a reflection of the interior of the house. It may be possible to position the mirror such that it reflects a nice view from another window, or an image of another room. Alternatively, or in addition, a screen might prove an ideal solution (*see* Figure 44),

Figure 43: Outside door opening onto stairs. Mirror can be used but of less significance

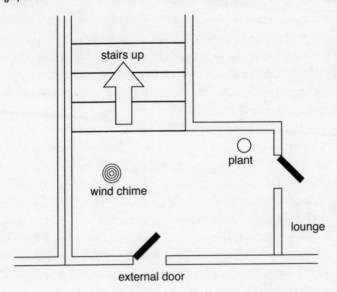

stairs up

plant

wind chime

lounge

external door

Figure 44: Possible use of screen and mirror to prevent escape of chi. Wind chimes could also be added

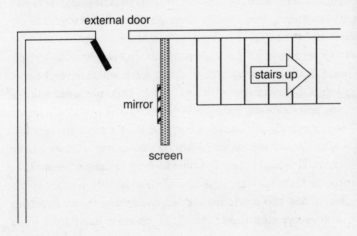

external door

stairs up

mirror

screen

providing a barrier to stop the escape of chi and enabling a mirror to be hung at an angle to the door thus providing a reflection of the inside. It is not a good idea to place a mirror immediately opposite the outside door, so that the first thing anyone entering the house sees is an image of themselves! Far better would be to hang a picture or something similar on the facing wall to present an interesting and attractive scene to whoever enters. A small porch with a door that leads directly to the door to a main room can cause an onrush of chi, and both doors should not be open at once. A series of two or more doors aligned and opening from one to another is very unfavourable, especially if one of these doors is the main entrance.

Another point to remember about entrances is that it is better not to fill a small area with furniture. Often one will see a telephone on a table, perhaps a chair, a bookcase and so on. It is not good policy to fill up the space by the entrance as if you were putting obstacles in the way of someone visiting. A clear, light and airy space is preferable, although the room leading from the main door should not be too large. If the available space is very small, or very narrow, the overall impression can be improved dramatically through the adoption of a light colour-scheme and relatively soft lighting.

Entrances often open directly into corridors or long hallways or even a lobby type of space from which several doors lead to the other rooms. It has already been mentioned that a long corridor with many doors leading off is not ideal and the corridor tends to channel the chi, making it move too quickly. Corridors are the means whereby chi moves to each of the rooms. It is important that the chi does not move too quickly and that it is not obstructed by items of furniture in the corridor. When the corridors and other common spaces such as landings are clear then the building is more likely to be filled with good chi. However, if there is a lot of awkward furniture to be avoided and generally a jumble of other bits and pieces the flow of chi is affected adversely and this has a knock-on effect upon each of the rooms, making the building, overall, a less welcoming and healthy place in which to live.

When corridors are particularly narrow, they are susceptible to the production of sha chi. The remedy is to prevent the chi flowing so quickly and in a straight line and this is best done by placing mirrors on the walls with the effect of creating a more wavy course for the chi. It has already been mentioned that hanging wind chimes or banners across the corridor will help. The problems associated with corridors tend, in the main, to be found in commercial office buildings rather than domestic homes. However, homes that do have an elongated design, particularly some one-storey buildings, may well have a long corridor that can be quite dark and stifling. Even so, there is much that can be done through the use of mirrors, wall hangings, subtle lighting and plants, providing space allows.

Very often the entrance hall, or a short corridor from the front door of a house, will lead first to the lounge or sitting room, and this is the room dealt with next.

The lounge

The lounge or living room, as the name suggests, is quite possibly the room where most time is spent and it is considered to be the room most yang in character. The bedroom and the kitchen, particularly if the latter is a dining kitchen, are also used a great deal but the lounge can be the most-shared room in the house. It not only serves as the gathering place for the family, whether watching television or just relaxing, but is also the focal point for socialising when friends are invited in for an evening. It will therefore benefit from being comfortable and welcoming, warm and light without being too bright and glaring.

A preliminary assessment of the room can be made by laying the Pah Kwa over the ground plan of the house. Then it will be possible to see in which of the eight sectors the rooms is situated. The grid is placed facing south irrespective of the direction of facing of the house and the location of the lounge can then be determined. Figure 45 shows the Pah Kwa superimposed upon the ground-floor plan of a real house with the different areas partially drawn in. The main door faces south east hence this is taken as the direction of facing of the house. It is interesting to note that prior to the addition of the porch some years ago, the door that now forms the entrance into the hall, was the main door and it then faced south west which would have generated a different analysis.

In this instance, the lounge falls within the areas of pleasure, and development and progress. This is a reasonable combination and quite appropriate for a lounge. It means that it lends itself to entertaining, socialising, and potential, whether it be discussing new plans and ventures or just capitalising upon forthcoming opportunities. There are certain stipulations and rules that some practitioners attach to this procedure but because of the outline of your house or the direction relative to the south facing Pah Kwa, it is not always possible to be absolutely accurate. However, it is perfectly possible to get a general idea of the endowments that apply and the likely outcome. Other directions that are favourable for the lounge are the south west, the area of contentment, where the feeling will be relaxed and settled, and the south east, which will provide an uplifting feeling. A lounge at or near the centre of the house is good, since this represents the heart of the home.

Ideally, the octagonal outline of the Pah Kwa should include two outside walls, the ones that are furthest apart, but

Figure 45

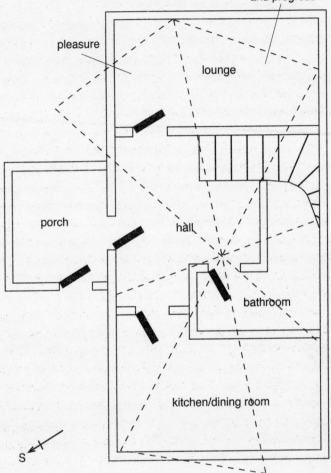

this is not always feasible. However, the extent of the octagon will cut walls at certain points and this gives an indication of the endowments that a particular room lacks or has in excess. In this particular example, there are extra areas for both the pleasure and development endowments indicating strengths in these aspects and although there is part of the pleasure area missing, the prospects for this room and the occupiers is good.

When applying the eight points to this room, the configuration is quite straightforward due to the rectangular nature of the room (*see* Figure 46). This means that no one aspect is exaggerated or diminished as would be indicated by a room extension or indentation. A square or rectangle is the most favourable shape for the layout of the lounge, and irregularities should be 'smoothed out' by the use of furnishing and other items. To correct a very irregular shape with sharp corners, fitted furniture would be ideal. There should be adequate but not cross-ventilation (*see* Inside Your Home/Window, page 124), the ceiling should be smooth without excessive design, and the floor level should not be lower than that of the rest of the house. The chi of a sunken floor can be brought up to the correct level with the use of plants and overhead lighting.

Figure 46

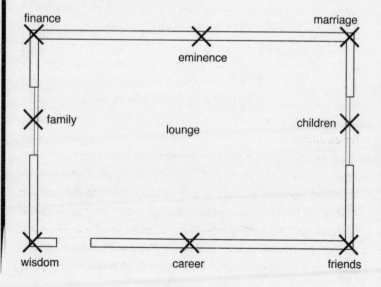

Figure 47

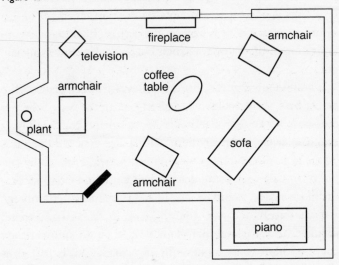

One of the many ways in which Feng Shui can help in the home, in addition to the placement of mirrors, and so on, to assist the correct flow of chi, is through the arrangement of furniture. There are a number of principles that can be followed when arranging furniture in this room. It can be focused around one of the eight points, preferably finance, marriage or friends. Finance and friends readily lend themselves to this plan as, in this room and many others, the location of these points in a corner is a natural focus. It is perfectly acceptable, for example, to place the television at the money point and for the furniture to be arranged accordingly (as demonstrated in Figure 47 in a hypothetical room). In this case, and this is always advisable, the chairs have been placed in order that the so-named 'honoured guest' position is facing the door, although not directly. The latter point is made because if this position faces the door directly it is rather confrontational and someone entering the room will face you, or your guest, directly rather than obliquely which leaves scope for choice in responses and movements. Note that the arrangement of furniture as shown here is well on the way to the octagonal configuration of the Pah Kwa which is a natural and pleasing layout.

The honoured guest position is nevertheless considered to be the best in the room and is often near to the fire, if there is one, and it would probably face the television comfortably. It may also face towards a window with a nice view although it is better to have an oblique view out of the window – to be facing it directly may create a feeling of being too exposed. It is the place a guest would be offered and it is almost certainly the armchair in which you would choose to relax. The general premise, and it is one that many people would automatically adopt without really looking for an explanation, is that armchairs and sofas have their backs against walls rather than against doors or windows. The reason is that this position may result in a feeling of insecurity; being placed against or near to a wall is more protective. Inevitably it may not be possible to place all seats with their backs to walls, but most rooms can probably accommodate this. However where a chair has to be placed next to a window, something in the window recess will help, a plant or a set of low bookshelves perhaps.

There are, in addition, a number of possible placements for the chairs and sofas, relative to each other. If chairs are placed opposite each other, even over an intervening low table, this obviously creates the situation where people are face to face, which may be fine for those who want to talk earnestly to each other, but not so comfortable for those who hardly know each other or who are not conversationalists (Figure 48). There is nothing worse than being seated opposite a garrulous person when you do not feel like talking or responding in like manner. Thus if the chairs or sofas are at right angles to each other

Figure 48: Chairs facing each other across the room [bad Feng Shui]

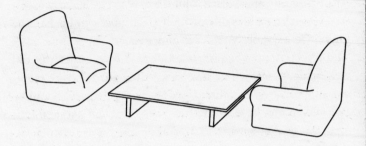

Figure 49: Chairs at right angles to one another [good Feng Shui]

there is more comfort in this layout and a person at the end of one sofa can enter the conversation when he or she wishes (Figure 49). Similarly, if the sofa and chairs are arranged as shown in Figure 47, basically with two chairs facing but at angles to the sofa, this is perhaps the configuration with which everyone can be happy. There is no need for directly facing another person and there is the option of directing comments to all or just one person.

The furniture you choose for your lounge will have an effect on the pace and nature of chi in the room (*see* Feng Shui Cures/Colour *and* Interior Decoration/Texture). A bulky three-piece suite in a small room will obstruct the flow of chi, causing listlessness where activity is required, especially if it crowds the centre of the room where empty space is desirable. An armchair or sofa with a rounded back is particularly auspicious, as it resembles one of the four symbolic animals – the protective tortoise. Armrests and a good supporting back 'embrace' the sitter, helping to produce feelings of security and well-being. A sofa with a low back will not provide the requisite support. It goes without saying that the chairs should be soft and comfortable so that the occupants and guests feel at ease. Hard chairs with sharp edges can direct cutting chi across the room, and may also increase restlessness by their activating yang nature. However, a sofa which is excessively soft could be too yin, and may inhibit communication or even induce sleep.

Fireplaces enhance the feeling of comfort and relaxation in the lounge and obviously of the five elements they represent the chi energy of fire. This is especially useful if the lounge is situated in the generally colder north or north east of the building. Even without a real fireplace, the fire element can be represented by a living flame gas fire, lighted candles or by certain patterns and colours (*see* Yin and Yang/The five elements, page 38). If the room in question has a number of alcoves, for example on either side of a chimney breast, then these can be improved by placing plants in the space to help the flow of chi. Lights are also useful in this respect, particularly if placed in conjunction with a painting hung on the wall. As mentioned previously, a tank of fish is considered very beneficial for activating chi. It is, however, important that a lounge does not become overfilled and therefore strewn with too many items of furniture, plants, ornaments and so on; the chi must be able to flow around quite easily, otherwise a feeling of laziness and apathy will be the outcome.

Many lounges are combined with a dining area in one room.

It is preferable that on entering the lounge, the dining room/area is not visible. If it is a dining area at one end of the lounge, it should be relatively easy to create a screen and this can be turned into an attractive feature, perhaps with plants and pictures of some sort.

CHECKLIST 4 Lounge/dining room
- Armchairs or sofas should not have their back to the door or window.
- The honoured guest position should not face the door directly; an oblique view of the window or door is ideal.
- Putting plants, lights or a fish tank in alcoves will help the flow of chi, but overfilling the lounge will produce a feeling of apathy.
- The dining room should ideally have no more than two entrances, nor should it have too many windows.
- If a lounge and dining room are combined, it is best to partition the dining area so that it is not visible on entering the lounge.
- The most auspicious placement of the dining table is at an angle to a rectangular room.

The dining room

Many of the general points mentioned for the lounge are also applicable to the dining room. The room should be arranged so that the chi can flow around easily and it should be made comfortable and familiar. The energising chi of the east is ideal for eating breakfast, while the west is good for evening meals, as it will have recently been energised. Ideally the room should be enclosed but if, as discussed above, your house contains a combined lounge-diner, then the dining area should be partitioned from the remainder of the room to create what is in effect a separate room. This can be achieved in an attractive fashion through the use of a wooden frame which may support climbing plants, pictures and mirrors; or through the placing of a unit of bookshelves or similar item of furniture. This creates the intimacy necessary and with a warm colour scheme, possibly different from the lounge itself, the overall feel will be very congenial.

It helps to have cheerful pictures and a fresh, light scheme of decoration (*see* Interior Decoration/Household accessories, page 189). While mirrors can be particularly useful for 'doubling' the size of food on a cabinet, suggesting abundance and wealth, it should be noted that too many mirrors are considered bad for this room, especially on the rear wall and where they reflect doors, staircases or toilets. Skylights and mirrors on the ceiling are to be avoided. Likewise, too many windows are unfavourable as they can cause uneasiness and distraction. However, this can be remedied by the use of lace curtains or flowers as discussed previously. It is best not to place the dining table next to a window or patio doors as this may result in an excess of yin energy from the cold and damp outside.

Whether the dining room is a separate room or a partitioned area, it should ideally have no more than two entrances. Doors should be kept closed when eating as an active flow of chi can make you hurry your meal. Inauspicious locations for the dining room include facing the main door, staircase or toilet, and directly above a septic tank or directly below a toilet. It should not be on a lower level than the kitchen or lounge.

The main item of furniture is, of course, the dining table and chairs. Although it is favourable for each chair to have its back to a wall, this is clearly not always going to be possible. Also, many would advocate placing an even number of chairs around the table as even numbers are considered very auspicious. This is probably due to the fact that pairs invariably conjure images of partnerships and love. However, if there are five members to your family, you will usually have an odd number of chairs around your dining table. Nevertheless, there are certain positions and placements of furniture that will create the most beneficial layout and allow the chi to flow readily around the room.

It would be avoided anyway, but the door on opening should not clash with the back of a chair. There is also an honoured-guest position in the dining room as there is in the lounge, again facing but not directly opposite the door. Very often the most auspicious placement is with the table at an angle to a rectangular room such that the table edges are not parallel to the walls. By placing the long edge of a rectangular table appropriately, it is possible to have two positions that would be considered honoured. In addition, it is beneficial if the general arrangement can be rendered to fit the octagon

Figure 50: Dining room configuration

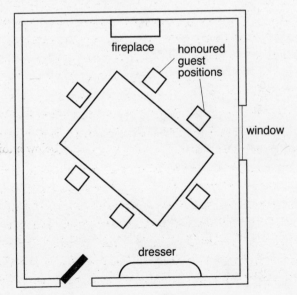

shape of the Pah Kwa but this may have to be represented in some other way. Of course, an octagonal dining table would be ideal! Figure 50 illustrates a basic arrangement. In this case the two seats facing the door are in the honoured position, no chair has its back to the window, and although two seats are placed with their backs to the door, which is not an ideal set-up, there is an oblique view through the window.

A slight modification is shown in Figure 51, with the table rotated a little more. This means that the second honoured-guest position is now somewhat more distant, but still valid, but it does mean that no-one is sitting with their back directly to the door. Once again, there are additional, small touches that can be made such as a vase of flowers in the hearth of the fireplace; and across the far corner of the room, either a mirror, decorative screen or something similar. In both these layouts, the table is sufficiently far away from them so as to cause no problem.

Figure 51: Alternative configuration for the dining room

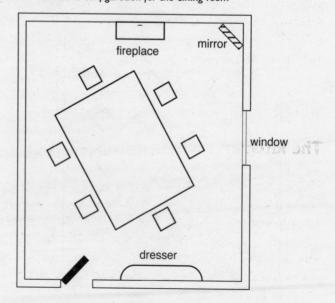

The dining room should be fairly limited in the other items of furniture contained – in addition to the table and chairs, some sort of unit, perhaps a dresser or sideboard, would suffice. Some rooms may possess a fireplace which provides a focus that, if not in use, can be decorated with flowers, a fan or an ornament. Table materials and shapes in themselves hold some significance. Wood is preferred for a wide range of uses, but different surfaces will produce different effects. A hard surface, such as glass, is generally regarded as unfavourable as it causes the flow of chi to accelerate – but this may be appropriate for business dinners, for example. When you wish to slow the flow of chi around your dining table – for an informal family dinner, for example – a tablecloth or place mats will help. The best material for chairs is also wood, and they should not have bars at the back which can generate arrows of chi.

The octagon, which has already been mentioned, is the most auspicious shape for your dining table. Referring back to Part I, a square table signifies the earth while a round one symbolises heaven. Of all the tables available only the rectangle and the oval present a position for the head of the table and are therefore considered more formal than other shapes (circle, square, etc) where there is no place for the head. For equality in a large family, a circular table is clearly the most suitable!

The kitchen

The kitchen is likely to be one of the busiest rooms in the house. In many homes, in addition to its primary function, the kitchen forms the social focus for the family and callers and almost everything happens there, especially if it is combined with a dining area that is used for day-to-day meals.

Clearly this is the room where food is prepared and it therefore represents the life of the household. It needs to be a room that can easily accommodate people going to and fro and yet provide all the necessary facilities for preparation of food, in a bright and if possible spacious area. The east and south east areas of your home are suitable for a kitchen, and the east is particularly suitable if it doubles as a breakfast room.

Although many modern kitchens are built in extensions to free up other rooms as living areas, this is unfavourable as it will be unprotected on three sides when it should be 'nurtured'. A kitchen in an extension should be 'reinforced' by fences, bushes and trees outside the house, which will provide a second external 'wall'.

The ideal position of being able to see whoever enters the room is not always possible in a kitchen when working at the cooker, sink or a worktop (Figure 52). However, providing the walls are not all covered with fitted cupboards, mirrors can be hung to counteract this problem and these will have the added benefit of making the room appear more spacious. The kitchen should not become a through way with constant traffic as this will disrupt anyone who is trying to work there. However, quite often and particularly in modern houses, the

Figure 52: Layout in which person cooking or washing dishes cannot see door

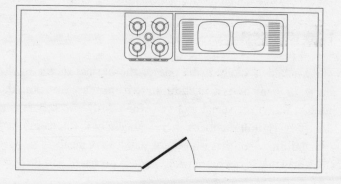

Figure 53: Encroachment into the kitchen

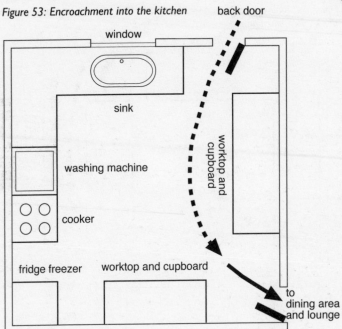

back door opens into the kitchen, so there is inevitably some conflict here. It may, however, be possible to create a passageway or walkway which helps to keep the kitchen self-contained (*see* Figures 53 and 54).

In Figure 54, the kitchen cupboard/worktop unit has been moved to create a natural route for anyone wishing to move between the kitchen door and the door to the lounge, and vice versa. This simple alteration can readily be accomplished and creates the self-contained space for the person in the kitchen while maintaining contact with all who enter, because the unit can be kept to normal worktop height.

In addition the diagram shows that by rehanging the back door to open in the opposite way, the person entering at the back door is naturally channelled into the 'passageway'. If they

Figure 54: Kitchen modification with improved flow and less disruption of the kitchen environment

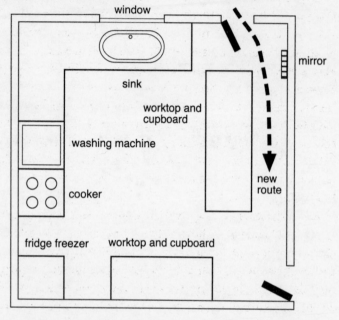

then wish to converse with whoever is in the kitchen, or enter the kitchen space, it is easy to do so. To avoid the feeling of confinement on entering by the back door, a mirror or two could be hung on the wall and if, as is the case in many modern houses, the back door contains some glass panels, then there is little detriment in having the door open in this way. There would be some benefit in this particular kitchen of placing one or two mirrors elsewhere notably above the washing machine and the unit on the same wall as the refrigerator/freezer.

It is interesting to consider briefly the influence that the five elements might have on the layout of a kitchen such as this. The elements in question are water (for the sink and the refrigerator) and fire (for the cooker). As mentioned earlier, there is a conflict between these two elements and the moderating influence is wood. It is considered best to avoid having the cooker placed opposite or next to the sink as this generates sha chi. This is also true of the refrigerator and washing machine, though to a lesser extent. The likely negative effects may include agitation, an argumentative family life or poor financial prospects. Because wood acts as the moderator between these two elements, then the situation can be remedied by inserting something relating to wood, which in terms of colours is something green. This could be wall or floor tiles of the appropriate colour placed between the appliances in question, an ornament of the same colour, a wooden table or a leafy plant.

When the kitchen door faces the front or back door, the chi may rush in and out without benefiting the room. It should be able to travel easily towards the room. If it is reached down a narrow, twisting corridor chi will have great difficulty reaching this room – and this is true too of clutter in the hallway or outside the kitchen door. This room should ideally have two doors to ensure the smooth circulation of chi. It is better to open the window every day to get rid of cooking smells rather than use an extractor fan, which simply rotates chi rather than removing the excessive yin chi associated with humidity. A cooker hood is acceptable, but an extractor fan should not be directly above the stove.

Essential to most food preparation, the stove is regarded by Feng Shui practitioners as one of the most important items in the house. A mirror placed on the wall above it will visually increase its size, and this is favourable. It also allows you to see who is entering the room when you have your back to the door, as mentioned. The stove should not be situated under a window as sunlight may affect the food and glass does not give the support a stove – as a central element of the house – needs. If the stove cannot be moved elsewhere, blinds or curtains should be kept closed while cooking.

It has already been mentioned that it is not favourable for you to have your back to a door while cooking. In particular, the stove should not be placed opposite an outside door as this will signify considerable loss of fortune. Any sha chi from external factors such as posts or roof ridges will be directed straight at this centre of life-giving activity. This can be remedied by placing a Pah Kwa or convex mirror outside the main door.

The stove should not be placed facing a toilet, with a toilet behind it, or with a toilet on the floor directly above as this will flush away your fortunes. The latter is particularly unfortunate as water chi travels downwards. The effects can be modified to some extent by placing a live plant in the bathroom and making sure the bathroom door is kept shut at all times.

Other bad locations for the stove are under a beam, in an island at the centre of the kitchen, opposite a staircase, across a corner, with a bed behind it, above a drainage or water pipe, facing the door of a bedroom and at the centre of the house. An Aga is preferable to gas, and gas is preferable to an electric oven. Microwaves are the least favourable, as they emit tiny amounts of radiation. Many Feng Shui practitioners will not install a stove without first checking with a consultant as to the timing. It is believed that carrying out work on the house on an inauspicious date is disruptive, but when an item, like the stove, is so central to the well-being of the householders it becomes even more important to get the timing right.

Also in the kitchen, units with rounded corners are necessary to avoid the risk of cutting chi, and cupboards are preferable to open shelves. You should check, in particular, whether potential sources of cutting chi are directed at the stove. The kitchen should have plenty of storage space so that surfaces do not become cluttered with utensils and laundry which will influence the chi of food preparation. Surfaces, which would ideally be made of wood, should also be kept clean, and the rubbish bin regularly emptied and kept out of sight, or sha chi may be generated. As with the dining room, some food – such as fresh fruit – can act as decoration, symbolising health and prosperity. Kitchen utensils should generally be kept out of sight. Chopsticks sticking out of a container are very inauspicious as they resemble the incense burned at Ching Ming, the Chinese Tomb Sweeping Festival. Knives should be kept in a drawer or knife rack, and never hung on the wall as they will cut through the positive chi of the room.

It is well worth your while trying to improve the Feng Shui of the kitchen as this is a much-used room and it contributes greatly to the overall well-being of the house and its occupants, not least because it is where food is prepared! As such, the kitchen is at the heart of family life and eating together as a family is a natural and constructive progression.

CHECKLIST 5 Kitchen

- Use mirrors to counteract the problem of not being able to see the door while cooking or washing dishes.
- The kitchen should not become a through way with constant 'traffic'.
- Chopsticks should not be stood upright, nor should the blades of knives be visible in the kitchen.
- The cooker should not be placed on an island in the middle of the room.
- Avoid having the cooker placed opposite or next to the sink and/or refrigerator as water and fire conflict.
- Kitchen extensions are inadvisable as they do not give the occupant much-needed 'support'.

At the Centre

Although this area has been covered briefly in other sections, it is worth mentioning that you should pay particular attention to what lies at the centre of your house. You will have worked out where the centre is by using your floor plan and Pah Kwa (*see* Assessing Your Building/Preparation and tools). It is unfavourable for a staircase, a toilet, a kitchen, a stove, an unroofed atrium, or too many plants to be located in the centre of your home (Figure 55). It is favourable for a lounge to be at the centre of your home, and this valuable area can be enhanced further by an item made of crystal, such as a chandelier. The centre of your house should be uncluttered, and if there is no furniture here so much the better – as empty spaces can actually encourage the flow of chi. You may apply a similar principle to each room in your house by trying to leave the centre free of furniture to promote circulation of chi.

Figure 55: Things to avoid at the centre of the house [bad Feng Shui]

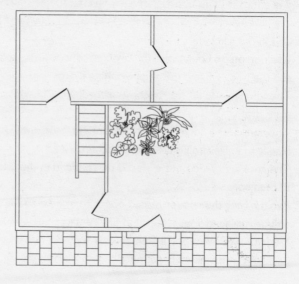

The Stairs

We have already mentioned some aspects regarding the location of stairs, in the section on the Entrance Hall. The main situation to avoid is stairs descending into the hall or that face the outer door directly leading to a loss of chi which suggests a loss of money (*see* Figure 25). It will also result in the rooms on the upper floor becoming depleted. In an apartment block, the main entrance facing the staircase will bring bad fortune to everyone in the building. This can be remedied to some extent in the manner discussed, with wind chimes, screens, mirrors and so on. Stairs that curve are good when it comes to the flow of chi and if the stairs curve away from the door towards the foot then this will prevent loss of chi (*see* Figure 56).

A staircase which faces the front door may be the least favourable location, but it is not the only one. According to Feng Shui principles, the staircase should not be located in the

Figure 56: Good layout of stairs for the flow of chi

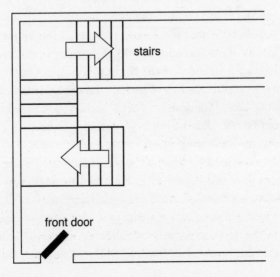

Figure 57: Stairs facing bedroom [bad Feng Shui]

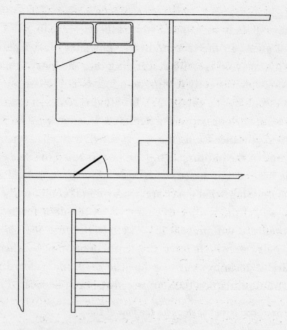

centre of the house because the movement of chi to the upper floor is a destabilising force and the heart of the house needs to be steady and to accumulate chi. A 24-hour light above the stairwell can help stabilise the chi in this case. A staircase facing a toilet signifies a loss of fortune, especially if the toilet is at the bottom of the stairs – as chi tends to flow downwards. This can be remedied by putting a curtain or screen in front of the door, or by hanging plants inside the bathroom. The staircase should not face a door at the top of the stairs, especially a bedroom door (*see* Figure 57). The same rule applies to apartment doors in relation to the main staircase.

In Figure 56 the stairs turn at right angles at two landings. The same effect can be accomplished equally well with continuously curving stairs. However, it should be mentioned that a spiral staircase is not necessarily the very good thing that it might at first seem to be. In this instance, the chi is likely to either move too quickly or be lost through the open risers in the stairs. Any staircase which have open risers will allow chi to escape. This can be offset by blocking the spaces in some way, although this could be difficult. Alternatively, a wind chime may help. A mirror would be ideal to reflect the chi back up but because this may be impractical, another solution may have to be found.

An additional potential problem with a spiral staircase is that it can be dangerous and generate sha chi. The corkscrew effect of a spiral staircase can have adverse effects upon certain aspects of your life. This can be offset by placing plants and lights underneath. A spiral staircase should never be carpeted in red as this symbolises the flow of blood from an injury caused by the 'corkscrew'.

There should preferably be enough space at the top and bottom of a staircase for chi to accumulate before circulating either up or down, and where the door and stairs are very close together a mirror should be placed over the door. At any rate, the stairs should be shallow and evenly spaced as sha chi may be generated if they are too narrow, straight, or uneven and irregular. Pictures, bright lights and a pale colour scheme can help to some extent, but if you place mirrors to deflect negative energy or to slow down fast-flowing energy make sure they do not 'cut the head off' anyone in your household.

Many Feng Shui practitioners also believe the number of steps – leading either to your front door or to an upper level of the house – can affect your fortune. The simplest way of working out whether you have the lucky number of stairs is to climb them, counting as you go. (A landing counts as one step, and you should count continuously to the top.) The four-step formula dictates that every third and fourth step in a four-step

153

cycle is bad. That means the third, the fourth, the seventh and the eighth steps are bad. The remedy for an unlucky number of steps is equally simple. If you are one step off a lucky number, simply place a mat at the bottom of the staircase and this will act as an extra step. If you are two steps off a lucky number, place another mat at the top of the stairs or on a landing. That mats should not slip or wrinkle on the carpet underneath goes without saying; otherwise they could prove very unlucky indeed!

CHECKLIST 6 Entrance halls/stairs
- A mirror should not be placed opposite the outside door.
- A very narrow corridor is susceptible to sha chi. To prevent the rapid flow of chi, mirrors, wind chimes or ribbons should be used.
- It is not ideal to have the front door opening into a small hall from which a staircase ascends, as it leads to a loss of chi, suggesting also a loss of money.
- Stairs that curve gently or turn at right angles at two landings benefit the flow of chi.
- Stairs with open risers lead to a depletion in fortune.
- A spiral staircase is inadvisable as it can generate sha chi.

The bedroom

This is clearly a very important room as we all spend a considerable amount of time here! It is also the most intimate of rooms and should be laid out and decorated in such a manner so as to present a calm, restful atmosphere and environment. Once again there will be the limiting factor of the room itself and its size and in most instances it will not be possible or desirable to undertake major reorganisation, involving structural alterations, to gain the most beneficial Feng Shui for your bedroom. However, there is much that can be done to enhance this room.

The general decor and colour scheme can be matched with the room – light, airy tones for a small room to create a feeling of space and freedom and stronger colours for a large room to make it feel more cosy and comfortable. In all cases there is a middle point, an optimum that can be found, and often this will coincide with the decor that a person with a good eye for colour would choose. If the view from the window is pleasant then this can be reflected into the room using a mirror, though care should be taken to place it correctly.

It will be useful initially to lay the Pah Kwa octagon over the room and indeed over the house floor containing the bedrooms. This will enable you to place the bed in the most positive area – perhaps family or pleasure. If, on laying the Pah Kwa over the whole floor, the bedroom falls within a less favourable endowment then it may be a good idea to move into another room with a more beneficial aspect. Checking the direction of the bedroom from the centre of the house will help you decide on an appropriate colour scheme. For example, a bedroom in the east may suffer from too much energising chi and, therefore, needs subduing with the appropriate decor (*see* Assessing Your Building/Symbolic animals, page 99).

When allocating rooms in the house, it is worth considering that according to Feng Shui principles, the bedroom door should not be at the end of a long hall and it should not face the door of another room, the bathroom door, the staircase, or a corner. The floor should not be lower than that of the toilet, the ceiling should not have a skylight – particularly over the bed. An en suite bathroom might seem like a good idea, but it can bring an excess of water chi into the room. The door to an adjoining should be kept closed, preferably with a screen in front of it.

Room shapes have been considered in earlier sections, but it should be noted that while irregular shapes are inadvisable for all rooms, they can be particularly bad for the bedroom. This is partly because you use one area of your bedroom – ie, the bed – for much longer periods of time than any other area of the house. Thus, the effect of, say, sha chi directed at your bed from sharp corners will be much greater than if it were directed at your dining table. Irregularities in the room are best ironed out by using fitted furniture – which is also the most practical way of utilising awkward space. It should be noted that an L-shaped bedroom is particularly inauspicious, since it resembles a cleaver and indicates a missing centre. If you cannot avoid sleeping in a room like this, you should situate the bed on the 'handle' and not the 'blade' of the shape. If the 'handle' is too narrow for a bed, place a large mirror along the whole wall here to 'extend' it to a more 'regular' shape. The mirror should not be in view from the bed. A plant at the corner will soften the edges in this case.

Figure 58: The position to avoid when putting a bed in a room

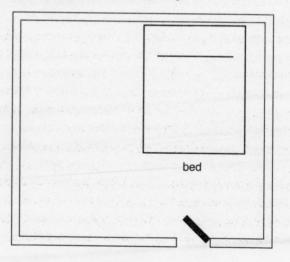

bed

The major item of furniture is of course the bed and there are a number of guidelines to consider with respect to its position in the room. The fundamental rule is to avoid the bed being placed with its foot directly opposite the door (*see* Figure 58). This particular position has connotations of death because in China this is the way, traditionally, that a dead person is laid out and the corpse is taken from the room feet first. However, it is preferable to see who is entering the room so in this case the bed could be moved to a side wall or placed across a corner. Figure 59 shows some other options, all of which would be satisfactory.

Of the four positions outlined in Figure 59, the oblique configuration across the corner, shown by the dashed line, may need something placed at the foot of the bed. This is because it is preferable to avoid chi flowing in through the door and straight over the bed as this can disturb sleep. Although the position in question does not allow direct flow of chi over the bed, a screen or plant placed at the foot will help. In any event, there are enough options in this room, but this remedy can be adopted where the options are limited.

Other configurations to avoid are with the foot of the bed directed to a window or with the bed head beneath a window, as this interrupts sleep and does not give the required 'support' to the person sleeping (Figure 60). A bed located between two doors will suffer from an onrush of chi from both sides (*see* Aspects of Life/Feng Shui for love). Furthermore, it is preferable to allow adequate space on the three sides of the bed for easy access. This assumes of course that a couple is sharing the bed.

The bed should not be situated between two columns or placed under a beam, shelves or cupboard, or in an alcove. All of these can put pressure on the chi, causing claustrophobia and headaches. Sleeping directly under an overhead light, a

Figure 59: Possibilities for good positioning of the bed in a bedroom

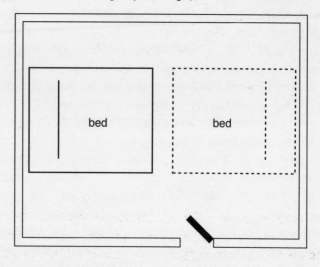

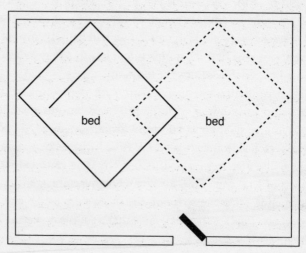

fan or where the roof rises to a point can also lead to head tension and lethargy. A stove, sink or toilet should not be placed on the other side of the wall. There are also a number of rules

Figure 60: Bed beneath a window [bad]

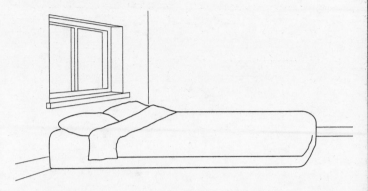

regarding furniture and water fittings on the floor directly above the bed (*see* Interior Decoration/Ceilings). The further the bed is from the floor, the less chi you are likely to receive, so sleeping on the floor, on a futon or mattress, is the most desirable position. In addition, clutter under the bed will block the flow of chi. The most favourable material for the bed is wood. Metal can speed up chi energy while a water bed will cause chi to stagnate. A round bed, associated with metal and movement, can cause sleeplessness. Ideally, the bed should have a 'protective' headboard, though not one with bars. When the head of the bed is against a wall, the headboard is less important.

Bedrooms contain other items of furniture: chairs, dressing table, wardrobes, sets of drawers, and so on. It is advisable to avoid overcrowding the room and to place these other items to complement the position of the bed. The areas immediately surrounding the entrance and the bed should, in particular, be free of clutter. Bookshelves, or in fact any open shelves, should be avoided as they can direct arrows of chi across the room, as can any triangular shaped or pointed objects. Electrical equipment, such as stereos, radio alarm clocks, televisions, and so on, should be kept to a minimum. A fish tank should not be placed

Figure 61: Bed reflected in two mirrors [bad Feng Shui]

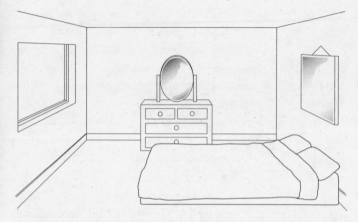

near the bed as this will energise the chi too much and cause restlessness. Pictures of water should be avoided for the same reason (*see* Interior Decoration/Household accessories, page 189). Tables, ornaments and windows which are round (thus representing movement and change) should be avoided, as should metal furniture, which gives off cold chi.

As mentioned, the atmosphere should be calm and since mirrors tend to stimulate chi, too many mirrors would be a bad thing. A dressing table usually has a mirror attached, and if placed sensibly, for example across a corner, it can work constructively in maintaining the steady flow of chi. A second mirror on the wall would be acceptable but it should not be placed opposite the dressing table mirror (Figure 61). If another mirror is required then it can be placed on the inside of a wardrobe door and used only when necessary. It is generally considered that a mirror is positioned so as to allow you to see yourself in bed will have a disturbing effect. Some Feng Shui practitioners avoid the use of mirrors in the bedroom altogether.

Whatever other pieces of furniture are placed in the room,

avoid aligning them in a way that leaves sharp edges directed towards the bed. Figure 62 shows a satisfactory arrangement taking into account the typical items of furniture to be included and the likely layout of a standard room. In this case the bed and dressing table are placed across two corners. This is only a practical solution if the room is sufficiently large, and in this instance the wardrobe could also have been placed across the third corner. This would be quite a good arrangement because the general layout would then have approached the octagonal shape of the Pah Kwa. Also seen in Figure 37 is the plant between the wardrobe and window. This both moderates the flow of chi and generates positive chi. A smaller room in which these three items (bed, dressing table and wardrobe) were flat against the wall would have worked perfectly well (*see* Figure 63). If the octagonal arrangement of the eight endowments is placed over this

Figure 62: *A satisfactory arrangement of furniture in a bedroom*

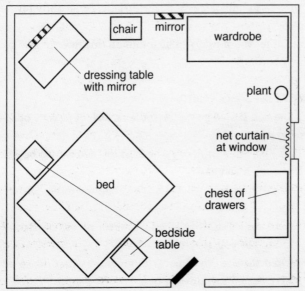

Figure 63: Layout for a small bedroom

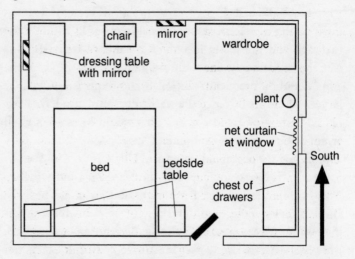

room it can be seen that the bed falls within the family/harmonious areas which is also good. For the effect of bedroom layout on romance, *see* Aspects of Life/Feng Shui for love, page 264.

The other room likely to be found on this floor in any house is the bathroom.

CHECKLIST 7 Bedroom

- The bed should not be placed with its foot directly opposite the door.
- Neither the foot nor the head of the bed should be placed beneath a window.
- Adequate access should be allowed to the three sides of the bed.
- It creates a disturbing effect if a mirror is positioned to allow you to see yourself in bed.
- Avoid aligning other pieces of furniture where sharp edges are directed towards the bed.

The bathroom

Some might consider this to be one of the most important rooms in the house, but it is often the one that is neglected. The physical arrangement of the components of the suite within a bathroom tends to be fairly standard and there is rarely any choice in the matter. When buying a house, the last thing you will want to do, unless this is in your plans anyway, is to completely rearrange the bathroom. However, the application of some basic principles will help.

The same guidelines apply here as in other rooms – whatever you may be doing, ensure that you can see anyone who may come in to the room. Now of course it is not generally very likely that someone will enter the bathroom if you are already in there taking a bath, a shower, or sitting on the toilet! Nevertheless, the same principles apply – be situated so that you can see everything from your position, which should be the best position in the room. This means that each item of bathroom furniture should be situated so that the person using it does not have his/her back to the door (*see* Figure 64).

Figure 64: Arranging the bathroom optimally

Figure 65: Preferred door opening for a bathroom

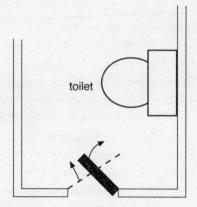

toilet

Certainly the toilet should not be the first piece of the bathroom suite seen on entering the room! In any event, it is customary practice when fitting a bathroom to avoid this situation and to have the door opening so as to 'cover' the toilet and not to expose it. Figure 65 shows the preferred direction of opening for the bathroom door (if it is unavoidable that the toilet be placed here); the dashed line represents the less satisfactory arrangement.

It is believed by many Chinese that chi will be lost down the waste pipe if the toilet lid is not put down. If your bathroom happens to be in the area representing money, then it may not be too surprising if your finances are not all you would wish them to be. Therefore be sure that the lid is always down and it also helps to keep the bathroom door closed.

The location of the bathroom is also considered by some to be important. It is preferable not to have the bathroom situated in the west or north east of the house plan. If this is the case however, it is good policy to decorate the room accordingly – earth colours of yellow, ochre, etc, for the former and all white for the latter. Also, bathrooms at the centre of the house are not a good idea because they negatively affect the chi of the whole house. If this is the case, you can place mirrors on the bathroom walls and on the outer side of the bathroom door. This keeps out sha chi and also activates chi inside the bathroom.

As mentioned in previous chapters, the bathroom should not be visible from or situated too near the main door, as the yin water chi will clash with the yang chi entering the house. It should not face a staircase or bed, nor should it lead from the bedroom, kitchen or lounge. This is one reason why en suites and open-plan apartments are not a good idea. Ideally, the bathroom should not be situated above a bedroom, main door or stove – as yin water chi travels downwards – nor should a toilet be immediately behind a bed in the house plan. The best place for a bathroom is in a less prominent position in the house, yet a large bathroom is good because the risk of stagnation of chi is much lower. Toilets which are in a separate room or section from the bath are highly favourable. The modern bathroom will often be at odds with traditional Feng Shui, because in ancient China, homes did not really have bathrooms at all.

The bathroom should have adequate ventilation and preferably natural light so that chi does not stagnate. Windowless bathrooms are the most hostile arrangement. Venetian blinds will let more light through a small window than curtains. As condensation and damp can build up in the bathroom, leading to a heavy and stifling water chi, keep this room clean, bright and dry. Mirrors are great for speeding up the flow of chi energy in a stifling room, but make sure they are not placed opposite one another. Furniture should be kept to an absolute minimum, and toiletries should be well-organised, preferably in a closed cupboard because clutter slows the flow of chi. Yang surfaces such as chrome and glazed tiles are ideal for stimulating sluggish chi; fabrics and wallpaper which strengthen the yin chi of water should be avoided (*see also* Interior Decoration/Texture, page 182 *and* Feng Shui Cures/Colour, page 88). Green, leafy plants will help absorb some of the humidity – and should thrive in this room.

CHECKLIST 8 Bathrooms
- Each item of bathroom furniture should be positioned so that the person using it does not have his/her back to the door.
- The toilet should not be the first piece of the bathroom suite to be seen on entering the room.
- If the bathroom is in the area representing money, the lid of the toilet should be kept down.
- The bathroom door should be kept closed at all times.
- If the bathroom is located in the west of the house paint it in earth colours and if it is placed in the north east decorate it in white, to offset any bad influences.
- A bathroom at the centre of the house can negatively affect the chi of the whole house, so place mirrors on the bathroom walls and outside the door.

Other rooms

Clearly, the basic principles of Feng Shui can be applied to every room in your house, especially with regard to doors, windows and furniture. In addition, there may be rules governing specific rooms which are equally applicable to rooms used for a similar function. The discussion on the bedroom above, for instance, should certainly be relevant to the guest room, while reference to the chapter on Feng Shui for business can be invaluable when coming to plan your own home office.

Nevertheless, it is worth looking in detail at some of the other rooms you might have in your home. These are:

- the home office/workshop
- the nursery
- the indoor swimming pool
- the exercise room
- the utility room
- the storeroom.

The home office

There is no Feng Shui principle that says working from home is a bad idea, but your choice of room and direction might influence your chances of success. The best place to locate your office is in the east of your home, which will help you to become more active and focused. Other favourable positions are south, south east, and north west of the centre. The rules for workshops are somewhat similar, but it is believed that a room in the north of the home is particularly good for academic study, the north east for creative work, the south west for practical work, such as DIY, and the south east for music practice.

The bedroom is the least favourable room in which to work. However hard you try to create an atmosphere conducive to both work and sleep, one area is likely to suffer as these functions have opposing needs. The best solution is to designate a room exclusively for use as an office or study but, failing that, designating a section of your lounge as office space is far better than attempting to sleep and work in the same place.

Obviously, the desk is the most important piece of furniture in the home office. While a large wooden desk will promote growth and suggest room for expansion, a small, cluttered desk will diminish your expectations. Opt for a desk which is oval

Figure 66

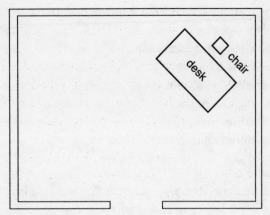

or, at the very least, has rounded edges, and if like so much office furniture your desk is all angles, use plants to offset the effects of potential arrows of sha chi.

As well as a good-sized desk, you should have a comfortable chair, though not so comfortable that you drift off to sleep every time you sit down to work! Cupboards are preferable to open shelves but, even so, your files and papers should be well-organised. Another Feng Shui concern is that you should only have as much electrical equipment as you need and this you should try to keep at a distance from your desk.

The ideal position for the desk is facing into the room with an unobstructed view of all doors and windows (*see* Figure 66). You should not be directly in front of a window as this will distract you from your work, nor should you have your back to the door. (*See also* Feng Shui for Business/In the Office, page 245.) It is best to use a room with plenty of natural light.

The nursery

The child's nursery often has the dual function of bedroom and playroom, so it must be stimulating by day and restful by night. A bedroom in the south east is ideal since it will promote activity without hindering sleep. A playroom in the east will encourage positive thought and activity, but should be balanced by a calming decor.

As has been noted elsewhere, mobiles can be used to stimulate chi in dull, dark areas (*see* Feng Shui Cures/Motion, page 94), but they will probably be too stimulating for the nursery at night. Mobiles should never be hung above the cot, as they induce sleeplessness. For the same reason, toys should be tidied away out of sight at the end of each day. Other causes of sleepless nights in children include placing the head of the bed beneath a window, leaving the door or curtains open, and clutter.

The indoor swimming pool

It may seem strange that so much attention is devoted to swimming pools in Feng Shui theories and guides regarding the home, but in Hong Kong and other regions where the practice of Feng Shui is popular, swimming pools – especially in apartment blocks – are not out of the ordinary. Although the home swimming pool is often seen as a sign of wealth, many Feng Shui practitioners believe that the strong yin effect of water can cause a severe depletion in finances. However, other practitioners attest to the Feng Shui benefits of a pool that is in the correct location and proportions. At any rate, a swimming pool actually within the family home is not ideal as the yin energy, not to mention the chemicals, can be overwhelming.

Living in an apartment block with an indoor swimming pool is certainly not the stroke of good fortune you might assume. Feng Shui practitioners are generally united in the belief that a swimming pool on the roof or ground floor of an apartment block is very inauspicious indeed. In addition, living directly above or below a pool is bad. Consider the remedial action that needs to be applied when a bath tub is located above your bed (*see* Interior Decoration/Ceilings), then compare this to the volume of water in an overhead swimming pool! When thinking of having a pool built, it is worth setting out all the options and, if possible, housing it in a separate building or braving the elements for a pool in the garden!

Within the home, a swimming pool should only be located in the east or south east of the building. The west is a particularly inauspicious location. The pool should always be filled with clean, filtered water, and the room must be well-ventilated or damp and corresponding negative chi will penetrate the rest of the house. As with the bathroom, it is necessary to keep the door to this part of the building closed.

The shape of your pool is also believed to influence your fortunes, and the same rules apply to Jacuzzis and outdoor pools. The size of the pool should be proportionate to the rest of the building or surrounding ground, and ideally curved or kidney shaped. A rectangle with rounded corners, an oval shape, or an irregular curved shape, are all suitable. Square and rectangular shapes with sharp corners, irregular pools with many corners, and L-shapes are all unfavourable. In addition, diving boards may generate arrows of sha chi.

All in all, if it's general good health you're after, the swimming pool might not be the best addition you could make to your home!

The exercise room

An alternative to the swimming pool, and a little less problematic, the exercise room is better placed in the active east of the house. Other suitable locations are the south east and the north east. If you exercise at home but do not have a spare room to allocate for your workout, it is better to use the lounge than the bedroom. This is because the yang chi needed for exercise is at odds with the calming purpose of the bedroom. Use bright yang colours to decorate this room; chrome would also be appropriate. Bear in mind the principles regarding heavy furniture, such as exercise equipment, being placed directly above beds, sofas and dining tables (*see* Interior Decoration/Ceilings). Be aware of machines with poles or sharp edges and, unless they can be placed so they are not directed at you when you are using another machine, minimise their effect with the use of leafy plants and well-placed mirrors.

The utility room

It is often desirable to keep heavy domestic equipment in a room adjoining the kitchen. As this room is likely to house appliances which produce yin energy, such as washing machines and freezers, the principles that govern the bathroom and the kitchen are relevant here. Ideally, the room should have plenty of fresh air and natural light, making good use of shiny yang surfaces such as glazed tiles and stainless steel to combat the likelihood of damp.

The storeroom

Sometimes a room is simply too problematic to use on a day-to-day basis. It may have no windows, a sloping roof, an irregular shape, or other factors that restrict the positive flow of chi. Rooms in the north east can be particularly difficult to match to suitable activities. In some cases, it may be better to turn the room into a boxroom for storage (Figure 67). Dark recesses and alcoves may also be converted into built-in cupboards. The important thing to remember is that even though the room may be closed off, the adage 'out of sight, out of mind' is unfortunately not applicable in Feng Shui. Clutter and storage are two entirely different concepts, and dirt or clutter can

171

Figure 67: A room without natural light [bad Feng Shui]

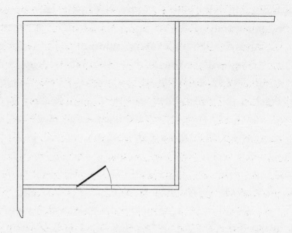

affect the chi of the whole house. Storerooms should be cleared out at least once a year.

Feng Shui for small houses

No practitioner of Feng Shui would try to claim that the ancient art is always consistent with the changing fashions of interior design. Thankfully, though, many principles of design are founded on 'common sense' which often, but not always, converges with the tenets of Feng Shui. Trying to live according to Feng Shui principles can be particularly frustrating for those who live in small houses or on a low budget, where even moving furniture or disposing of a potential source of sha chi might not be practicable. Therefore, this section briefly summarises those practices outlined in previous chapters that might be useful to the small householder. In addition, readers who live in certain homes might like to refer to the sections on high rises, shared corridors and terraces (Outside Your Home/Building types, page 204).

In some houses, instead of a hallway a small porch will lead directly into a main room, usually the lounge. This is regarded as unfavourable because chi will enter the room too quickly, and Feng Shui consultants generally advise clients with this type of house or flat, to place a screen or partition just inside the room. Clearly, this is not practical for anyone with a very small room, but it is almost as effective to make sure the doors are never open at the same time and to place a cloth or bead hanging over the inside door. When certain rooms are facing other rooms or if there are too many doors, the use of screens and partitions is also suggested as a way of offsetting the ill-favoured location. Again, a door hanging can work quite well; an automatic closer fixed to the door is also helpful.

In Feng Shui it is considered necessary for there to be some space for chi to accumulate before it ascends or descends the stairs. If your landing or hallway is very small, or the staircase is located too near the main entrance, placing a mirror on the front door will create the illusion of a much larger space. Small entrance spaces should be kept absolutely free of clutter, with bright lighting to stimulate the chi. As some rooms have only one door, instead of the recommended two, the chi will have to use the same entry and exit point. To encourage chi in this type of room, it is possible to have recourse to one or more of the eight cures, outlined earlier in the book.

Open-plan flats are not well-regarded by Feng Shui consultants due to the likelihood of conflicting areas or doors facing one another. The use of partitions is strongly advised, especially when the kitchen and lounge are adjoined. This is often achievable, even in a small flat, as a screen will in effect create an extra wall along which you can place small items of furniture. A wall made out of glass bricks is an ideal way of dividing a room if the kitchen area has no window of its own or if a screen would create dark corners. Where a partition is not possible, you should at least keep the kitchen area clean and free of cooking smells, with a regular supply of fresh air. A view of dirty dishes from your armchair will not promote a relaxed atmosphere! The artful placement of furniture can divide a room effectively, and even a low cabinet with potted plants will have some effect.

In order to make maximum use of space, some bijou flats have split-level rooms. These tend also to be popular with interior designers, but are not thought of highly by Feng Shui consultants. At any rate, areas for socialising should never be higher than bedrooms or home offices as this elevates the status of guests above that of the householder. There seems to be some debate as to whether a mezzanine is regarded as a floor for Feng Shui purposes. A bed should not be too high off the floor, otherwise chi will have difficulty reaching it, but obviously a mezzanine floor is to be preferred to a bed elevated on posts.

Additional recommendations regarding the bedroom can be found in the relevant section (*see* Inside Your Home/The bedroom, page 154), but the most important point is that the foot of the bed should never be directly opposite the door. Where this is not possible, placing a screen or a plant at the foot of your bed will help. Obviously, trying to arrange your furniture in a Pah Kwa pattern is not practicable in a small house (*see* Figure 29), and a bedroom in which the furniture is placed against the walls is perfectly acceptable (*see* Figure 63). As fitted furniture often makes better use of space than free-standing, filling in any irregularities with made-to-measure cabinets or wardrobes serves a dual function: it will iron out the shape of your room, benefiting the flow of chi and eliminating the possibility of sha chi from sharp corners; it will also turn awkward, unusable space into storage, freeing up more useful space elsewhere.

There are also many simple interior decoration techniques as well as small household accessories that you can use around your home to offset negative influences. These are considered in the next chapter.

Interior
Decoration

Feng Shui is not just about improving your existing environment or applying remedies to unfavourable situations. You should be aware that anything you do to your immediate surroundings – from planning an extension to moving the furniture to hanging a new picture in your bedroom – will influence the balance of chi around you. Unknowingly, you may be working towards a more harmonious atmosphere for your family but, equally, you might be disrupting the ideal conditions for your home, or even removing a natural antidote to harmful sha chi. Before renovating, decorating or even buying a new bookcase, it is worth assessing the possible effects of your actions.

Renovation

As the biggest alteration you are likely to make to your home, renovation is a good place to start. Obviously, it is also the alteration most likely to have significant impact on the atmosphere of your home. Before embarking on any major work, it is vital that you draw a new floor plan which incorporates the proposed renovation, using the Pah Kwa to ascertain how the changes will affect the dynamics of your house (*see* Assessing Your Building/Preparation and tools, page 107). If the indications are unfavourable, you should consider making alternative arrangements.

Extensions usually have considerable effect on the chi in a house for three reasons. Firstly, an extension generally means that the centre or focal point will move. If the centre moves to a less favourable location, such as the toilet, for example, this will allow the good fortune – gained from a former auspicious siting, perhaps – to drain away (*see* Inside Your Home/At the centre, page 150). If a negative element was previously situated at the centre of the house, however, an extension may prove useful.

Secondly, an extension will change the shape of your house which, if your house was a perfect square or rectangle before, may be negative. L-, T- and U-shapes are particularly unfavourable (*see* Outside Your Home/Building shapes, page 198). Even if the extension does not significantly alter the shape, it will make itself felt to the various occupants, depending on which side it is added to (*see* Outside Your Home/Protrusions and indentations, page 201).

Thirdly, some extensions – such as a new porch or conservatory – can alter the facing direction of the main door (*see* Figure 45), and whether this change in direction will be a weakness or a strength can be calculated by using the Pah Kwa. You need to consider how renovation work might change the dynamics inside the house, including the position of the doors and the relation between rooms, as well as what building materials you should choose for each different area. These considerations are dealt with in detail in other sections.

Specific renovation work will involve additional questions. For example, a loft extension should be planned carefully for a number of reasons. Many loft apartments and attic rooms have sloping ceilings, exposed beams and skylights. This can affect the balance of chi in the room, and is especially unfavourable for a bedroom (*see* Interior Decoration/Ceilings, page 185). The design of the staircase to the attic is important, as spiral staircases in particular have a tendency to generate sha chi (*see* Inside Your Home/The stairs, page 151). You should also consider how a loft extension may change the shape of your roof (*see* Outside Your Home/Building shapes, page 198).

Sun lounges and conservatories are very popular, and are a great way of bringing natural light into the home, thus encouraging the circulation of chi. However, many conservatories have pointed roofs and sharp ridges or beams between each individual pane of glass. This is a sure way of generating sha chi, and as many conservatories are used for relaxing – sometimes for hours at a time – it can have damaging effects on the health of the user (*see* Interior Decoration/Ceilings, page 185). A rounded conservatory with a dome-shaped roof is ideal, but if it constitutes an unfavourable protrusion (*see* Outside Your Home/Protrusions and indentations, page 201), it would be far better to build a small gazebo at a distance from the house. While it may seem like a decided asset, a home swimming pool can engender too many problems to be workable (*see* Inside Your Home/Other rooms, page 166). Even the humble shed should be planned in a way so as not to direct arrows of chi at the house or to block a source of sheng chi from the natural surroundings.

After using the Pah Kwa and floor plan to find the best location, size and building materials for the renovation work, there is one more point worth considering. Most Feng Shui practitioners would only begin renovation on a certain day after consultation with a geomancer, as it is believed that opening up areas, knocking down walls, and banging, drilling and sawing can destabilise chi in the home. Starting on an inauspicious day can lead to all sorts of delays and problems in the process. It is also believed that renovation should not begin at all when one of the occupants is pregnant. Even if it is a much-needed nursery that is being built, many practitioners believe it should wait until the baby is born.

Walls, ceilings and floors

It is now widely recognised that the colours you surround yourself with can have a profound effect on your moods and your relationships, as well as sending out messages about what type of person you are. Feng Shui consultants have been saying this for centuries, but while people are becoming more conscious of colour choices, they often do not realise that the materials they use in their home will also influence the nature of chi in their home. In fact, an area of the home that is too yin or too yang for its purposes can be redressed to some extent by the type or texture of the materials you choose for your walls, floors and furnishings.

Texture

All types of glass, metal and shiny, glazed tiles are yang, increasing the speed at which chi flows and thus most suited to areas where it tends to stagnate. The use of chrome in a bathroom, particularly if it is situated to the north of the house, is ideal. Polished stone such as marble also speeds up the flow of chi, but should not be used in bedrooms where it may cause restlessness. The uneven texture of a softer stone such as slate will disperse the chi, and can be useful in areas which lack natural light such as bathrooms and storerooms. Unglazed terracotta tiles are yin, and slow the movement of chi.

Wood does not generally affect the flow of chi, and can be used throughout the house, though it is most beneficial in the north, south and east. The smooth, polished surface of mahogany, however, will speed up the flow of chi, while the soft, rough texture of pine will slow it down. A sanded or parquet floor is ideal for the bedroom, where the surface should be smooth and even. A plain carpet is also suitable for this room.

It is no coincidence that many people make abundant use of heavy curtain fabric, rugs, pile carpets, and soft furnishings in the lounge, for such materials slow the movement of chi, producing a suitably relaxing atmosphere. However, overuse will cause chi to stagnate, leaving a dense, dull quality to the room. Natural fabrics, such as cotton, silk or wool are ideal, and felt underlay is preferable to synthetics. The use of synthetic material in general should be kept to a minimum, as it can obstruct the flow of chi altogether.

Increasingly popular plant fibres for floors, such as rush or sea-grass, are extremely yin and work in much the same way as fabric. However, they also collect dust which can have negative effects on the flow of chi. Natural fibres such as bamboo, wicker and rattan, used mainly for furniture but also for blinds and mats, have similar properties.

In general, matt surfaces will slow the flow of chi, creating a yin atmosphere which will be best-suited to the quiet areas of your home, while shiny surfaces will speed up the flow, creating a yang atmosphere, suited to the areas in which you work or socialise. However, you also need to assess the existing flow of chi in a room before you attempt any remedial action. Will you need materials that maintain, enhance or decelerate the flow of energy? To assess this, you need to look not only at the purpose of the room, but which direction it lies in your home, and to observe any other features which might affect the flow of chi (*see* Inside Your Home, page 111).

Floors

Most people do not devote nearly as much attention to their floors and ceilings as they would their walls. However, just because they are not as conspicuous as walls, it does not mean you can afford to ignore these areas. As a general rule, the pattern of your carpets should be harmonious and balanced. A crazy-cut pattern on linoleum is inadvisable, for instance, as it can cause a feeling of disorder and confusion. Uneven floor surfaces contribute to a feeling of personal difficulty, while an over-polished floor may make you over-cautious – though this may not be a bad thing in the home of a compulsive gambler! Lines formed by tiles or wood should not cross the front door

Figure 68: Floorboards crossing the path of the main entrance [bad Feng Shui]

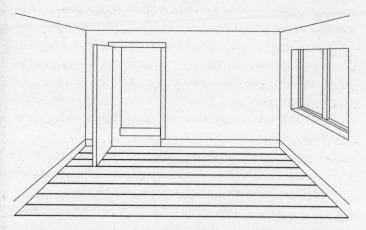

as this presents an obstacle to chi and makes for an unwelcoming home (*see* Figure 68). They should instead run from the door into the house, helping to draw the chi inside (*see* Figure 69). The factors which decide floor surfaces are discussed in Interior Decoration/Texture, page 182.

Figure 69: Floorboards running from entrance into the house [good Feng Shui]

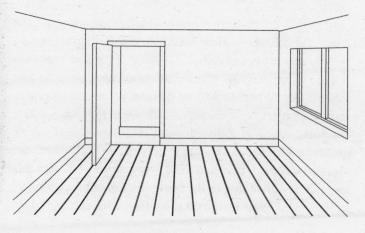

Ceilings

The best ceiling is one which is smooth and whose height suits the proportions of the room. Low ceilings can create oppressive energy, but this can be remedied to some extent by using white or light pastel colours to create the illusion of space, as well as making sure the surface is smooth and even., with overhead lighting flush to the ceiling.

Columns with sharp corners, cornices with acute angles, and irregularities which create more corners or recesses all increase the possibility of arrows of chi harming the occupants. Fill larger recesses with built-in furniture or plants, and round off sharp protrusions or place plants in front of them. It has already been mentioned that a mirror should never be placed on a ceiling, especially above the bed where seeing yourself lying prone can subconsciously suggest ideas of sickness to you.

Exposed beams are regarded as harmful as they exert pressure on anyone unfortunate enough to spend time underneath them. A beam which crosses the threshold of your home will, in effect, block chi from entering, with a corresponding restric-

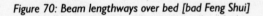

Figure 70: Beam lengthways over bed [bad Feng Shui]

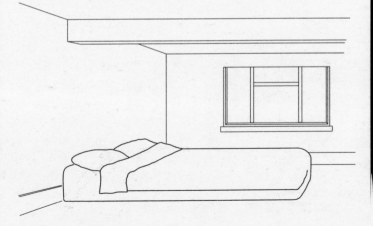

tion of your fortunes. Sitting under a beam for any length of time will cause headaches and lapses in concentration. Thus a sofa, desk or bed should never be situated under a beam. In addition, a beam running lengthways above a dining table will cut the energy field into two, causing family rifts and failed dinner parties. If it is impossible to move the table, a light can be hung from the beam to diffuse the weight of the chi. As the stove is central to the well-being of the household, you should avoid placing this under a beam. While a beam running widthways over a bed can cause a number of ailments, one which runs lengthways down the centre of a couple's bed can ruin their love life as they keep to their own sides of the bed to avoid its pressure (*see* Figure 70). If you really cannot move the bed elsewhere, the ceiling should be lowered to the level of the beam, at least above the bed (*see* Figure 71).

With loft space becoming an increasingly popular alternative to buying a new home, sloping ceilings are now commonly used in architecture. In fact, a sloping ceiling creates an imbalance of energy by directing the flow of chi to the lowest point. If that

Figure 71: Beam widthways over bed, corrected by lowered ceiling [modified Feng Shui]]

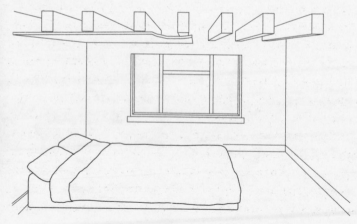

Figure 72: Ceiling sloping towards the door; chi rebalanced by wind chime [modified Feng Shui]

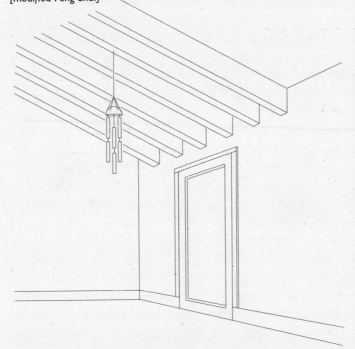

point also happens to be where the door is situated, energy will be depleted as it pours out of the room whenever someone enters. When levelling the ceiling is not an option, a wind chime should be hung from the lower end of the ceiling to redistribute the accumulating chi (*see* Figure 72). Try to avoid sleeping in a room with a sloping ceiling, particularly if this is combined with exposed beams.

Knowing what is on the floor above you is also important, though this can be difficult if you live in a flat. It is preferable not to sleep with any heavy item on the floor directly above your bed, but in all other areas of life, the effects of heavy electrical goods or furniture, such as air conditioners, pianos and

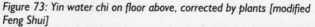

Figure 73: Yin water chi on floor above, corrected by plants [modified Feng Shui]

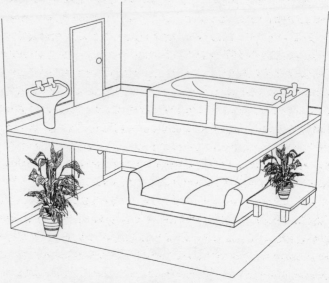

exercise equipment, can be minimised by hanging a wind chime from the ceiling immediately beneath the object. Negative yin energy from water tanks, bath tubs and washing machines can be offset by placing plants on a stand underneath them (*see* Figure 73).

CHECKLIST 9 Interior decoration/general

- Use glass, polished hardwoods, stainless steel and glazed tiles on your floors or walls to speed up the flow of chi; use sea-grass, rattan, terracotta and fabrics to slow it down.
- Too much plastic in your home will block the flow of chi.
- Make sure you do not sleep, work or relax underneath any exposed beams, as this can cause headaches, lapses in concentration and even marital problems.
- A wind chime should be hung from the lower end of a sloping ceiling to redistribute the flow of chi.

- Try to avoid placing your bed where there is a bathroom, electrical goods or heavy furniture on the floor immediately above.

Household accessories

There is more to good Feng Shui than having the right furniture in the right place. In interior design, it is often the details that count and likewise in Feng Shui the placement of decorative objects, such as pictures and ornaments, and items for use, such as clocks and kitchenware, can enhance or diminish the level and type of chi in your home. Although the use of certain household accessories, such as mirrors, light and plants, have been dealt with in previous sections (Feng Shui Cures, page 81), there are other symbols of good fortune which, when displayed prominently, should help you attract positive chi.

Pictures

Works of art operate on a number of levels. The colour of a painting will relate to one of the five elements and may be more suitable for some areas of the house than others (*see* Feng Shui Cures/Colour, page 88). As each colour conveys something of the element it is related to, such as green for wood and silver for metal, clashing colours will result in a confused emotional state. When placed in the bedroom or office, this type of painting can cause conflict while dull, lifeless colours will induce depression and lethargy. The texture and materials, especially in sculpture, will also suit certain areas of the house more than others (*see* Interior Decoration/Texture, page 182). Of central importance is the subject matter of the artwork and whether it has any symbolic value. Pictures of lucky items or one of the four celestial animals (*see* page 100) may subtly increase good

189

fortune. The symbolic meaning of flowers is considered in a later section (*see* Designing Your Garden/Flowers, page 235).

Pictures which depict natural disasters or violence, poverty or despair can lead to anxiety and fatigue; while pictures of grotesque or distorted body parts can cause tension and headaches. Portraits of ancestors and even posters of celebrities who have died should not be displayed in the bedroom, as they produce an excess of yin chi. Provided the colours are well-balanced, abstract paintings will revive dull areas. While Chinese calligraphy has wide appeal, promoting intellectual development in much the same way as books and maps, you should take care to understand what the characters mean. Calligraphy is best placed in the study.

Landscape paintings which depict a road or river should provide an entry point into the room rather than an exit. This means that a person or vehicle in the picture should be facing the room, not moving away from it. However, the person should not seem to be walking towards door or window of the room. It is favourable for water to 'flow towards' your desk, as it corresponds with money, but it should not 'flow' from behind a chair, or out of a window or door. Pictures of mountains are well-placed behind a study chair, however, as they reinforce a feeling of support and solidity. Water landscapes should not be hung in the bedroom, particularly above the bed, as the movement represented by this element is too energising for sleep. Pictures of light-filled houses and gardens promote a sense of security, and are ideal for most areas of the home, although they should not contain too many birds or other symbols of flight. The best pictures for the dining room are paintings of gardens or still-lifes. Fruit and other food items are, of course, ideal subjects for this room. If you have any doubt about the effect of a painting, you should place it in an area of your home used only for entertaining.

Ornaments

As with pictures, the symbolic meaning of ornaments will also inspire certain feelings in you. A round-edged sculpture of a family promotes harmony and security, for example. Different shapes, colours and materials will also have different effects – as discussed in previous sections (*see* Yin and Yang/The five elements, page 38; Feng Shui Cures/Colour, page 88; *and* Interior Decoration/ Texture, page 182). Wooden animals should be placed in the areas of the home most conducive to activity; for example, the east; square boxes and clay birds should be used in areas where stability is desirable; while glazed ceramics and round objects should be placed in the study where concentration is required. Jade, which functions as a symbol of protection (provided it is bought for you by someone else), also enhances concentration.

Antiques

In Chinese Feng Shui, it is vital that the origin of any second-hand items you bring into your home is known, as they carry the chi of previous owners and past events. In addition, heavy antique furniture may cause lethargy if it obstructs or slows the flow of chi, is dark in colour, or is placed directly above an area in which you work, rest or sleep (*see* Interior Decoration/Ceilings, page 185). Too much furniture which belongs to the element of wood, for example, can tip the balance of a room unfavourably towards that element. However, it may also be useful to decelerate the flow of chi in certain areas (*see* Feng Shui Cures/Static elements, page 94), and sturdy furniture and large antiques may have a grounding effect when a career or relationship is unstable. Heavy ceramic vases should be moved from time to time.

Animals

The key to using any lucky object, in the form of a picture or ornament, is where you place it. The four symbolic animals, tortoise, phoenix, dragon and tiger (*see* Assessing Your Building/Symbolic animals, page 99), serve as lucky objects for certain purposes, but will only really enhance your luck if located in certain places.

A symbol of longevity and security, the tortoise may be suitable for an older person's room but should not be placed in the office where greater activity is required. As a symbol of authority, the dragon is ideally situated in your home office but is also appropriate for the lounge. It should not be positioned to face the door or a window. Representing courage and strength, the tiger can also be placed in an office, but should not look as if it is about to pounce. It should be lying down and facing away from the door. Amber, which symbolises the soul of a tiger, can be used as a substitute, but as it belongs to the fire element, care needs to be taken in finding a suitable position. The phoenix, which stands for renewal, brings good fortune when it is situated near the front of the house, although it should not look as if it is flying towards the door.

Two other creatures thought to bring wealth and good fortune are the frog and the fish. These can be found on many ceramic objects, such as vases, bowls and even kitchenware. Ideally, a fish symbol should be placed on the table in the lounge or near the front entrance. The frog is often placed near the main entrance, but it does not need to be in a prominent position if you really can't bear to look at it! Other lucky animals are the mythical unicorn (sometimes referred to as the dragon horse) and the peacock.

Clocks

Clocks are sometimes used by Feng Shui consultants in areas of the home where it is thought that the movement of the clock's hands will stimulate the circulation of chi. The best shape for your clock is oval, hexagonal or octagonal. It should be placed on the dragon wall or on the front wall of a room, but should not face the main door. As clocks are also a reminder that time is running out, they should not be given as house-warming gifts.

Maps and books

Maps and books displayed prominently encourage you to extend your knowledge, although maps which are out of date bring bad luck by misleading you as to the geography of the land. As with all items in your home, it is better if you know where your maps and books have come from. You should also be aware of what your books contain.

Kites

Symbolising energy, activity and social and intellectual development, kites should not be stored in cupboards but made full use of in household decoration. Chinese kites, often in the shape of a dragonfly or butterfly, can be an attractive accessory for the wall and, in a nursery, they will coax the child outdoors and towards learning. Kites are also a symbol of personal development, ambition and growing wealth.

Shells

Shells not only bring a touch of the sea to those who are landlocked, they also represent money. When placed in the money area of the home or of a certain room, shells can increase the fortune of the occupants. As with any item, they should be clean and dry, however.

Toys

Many adults keep the toys they played with as children. In Feng Shui, it is considered very unfavourable to keep unused dolls and stuffed toys, especially if they are dirty or tattered. Toys which you cannot bear to part with should be washed and dried, and stored away neatly. In a family home, toys are important – but must be tidied away at night. Some Feng Shui consultants believe one or two well-placed toys may help childless couples to conceive.

Outside
Your Home

When contemplating moving house, the opportunity arises to apply Feng Shui in a beneficial way, in much the same way as we improve a house through interior design and decoration – as indicated in the previous section. The location and direction of facing is relevant, as is the type of structure in which you live. If a move is not imminent, then it is worth considering anyway, so that remedies can be applied wherever possible.

Direction

Depending upon the direction in which your building faces, there will be a different type of chi trained upon your home. It is necessary to look around your immediate area to see whether the Feng Shui of both the natural and the man-made environment is good or bad. There may be four types of chi involved: yang chi from the south; t'sang chi from the north; sheng chi from the east; and sha chi from the west.

As we already know sha chi is disruptive, so it is important to see whether there is any way in which it can enter the west-facing doors and windows of your house. If there is some possibility of this happening when they are open, then counter-measures must be employed, such as a mirror opposite the door if the main door is on the west – although this is not always the most favourable position for a mirror (*see* Inside Your Home/Doors, page 113). This will reflect the sha chi back out. Also, windows on the west side of the house can be susceptible so chimes or similar hanging ornaments will help, as will plants.

The remaining types of chi are more helpful and creative: sheng chi provides creative energy; t'sang chi or hidden chi induces relaxation and sleep; yang chi is nourishing. In Feng Shui, direction is also represented by the four symbolic animals (*see* Assessing Your Building/Symbolic animals, page 99).

197

Building shapes

It is not only the orientation of a house or office building that is important, but also the shape. That is because each shape will belong to one of the five elements, and chi will always assume the qualities of the particular element (*see* Yin and Yang/The five elements, page 38). This also applies to the shape of apartments. In assessing your own house or workplace, you will need to consider the shape of the surrounding buildings, and their corresponding element, as this will have a direct impact on the Feng Shui of your own. If your house has an irregular shape and thus represents the water element, and if it is in a neighbourhood dominated by the tree energy of tall, thin buildings, you and the other occupants of your house may suffer from a depletion of energy as the tree element drains water. In this section, we will look simply at the implications of your own building shape. The interaction between the different elements and the solutions to unfavourable combinations, are discussed at some length in an earlier section (*see* Yin and Yang/Moderating elemental conflicts, page 55 *and* Figure 14).

A square house is the most favourable building shape you could hope for, especially if you have a family, because it belongs to the earth element and thus the chi will assume the qualities of solid strength. A rectangular shape also belongs to the earth element, and will be auspicious if the narrow side faces the street, indicating a long future for the occupants. The reverse will be true, however, if the wider side faces the street. Likewise, the earth element brings security to the occupants of a trapezoidal house if the wider side is at the rear, as the rear of the house can represent the future. The reverse is true if the wider side faces the front. Possibly the only combination of shapes that is more beneficial than one which belongs to the

Figure 74: Favourable building shapes [good Feng Shui]

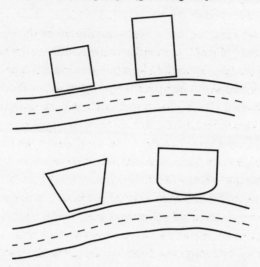

earth element, is a square which has a semi-circular section at the front. As a mix of the earth and metal elements, this is considered particularly fortunate as it promotes both the safety and the wealth of the occupants (*see* Figure 74).

The triangular shape belongs to the fire element and is regarded as unsuitable for rooms, houses or office buildings. It is probably the most anti-social house shape you could choose, as it will emit arrows of chi which are directed at your neighbours, bringing them bad fortune unless they apply Feng Shui remedies themselves. Even if you did wish harm to your neighbours, as is sometimes the case when rival businesses are located in the same area, any corrective measures they take could be directed straight back at your own. Furthermore, the generation of sha chi can cause friction and general bad feeling in a neighbourhood, and this will make itself known in your home or business too.

Other unfavourable shapes include the circle which belongs

to the metal element, representing movement and thus lacking the stability needed for home life, though it can reap great rewards for financial institutions. Dominated by the wood element, a very narrow rectangular house also lacks the stability which makes the regular earthy rectangle so suitable for houses. A narrow house also increases the prospect of fast-flowing sha chi to circulate. Belonging to the water element, the yin chi of an irregular shaped house can cause health problems for the occupants (*see* Figure 75). An L-, T- or U-shaped house might not always be unfavourable if the shape is not too exaggerated, but the heart of a house functions as its centre of gravity, helping to keep the occupants united. If the centre of gravity is outside the house, as is often the case with the 'L', it will cause problems for the family that lives there. A swimming pool located between the two wings of a U-shaped house can have disastrous consequences as water chi will permeate every area of the building, leading to sickness, laziness and depression.

Figure 75: Unfavourable building shapes [bad Feng Shui]

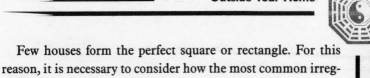

Few houses form the perfect square or rectangle. For this reason, it is necessary to consider how the most common irregularities in the form of protrusions and indentations affect the Feng Shui of your home.

Protrusions and indentations

Many houses have indentations or protrusions which not only makes the division of the house for Feng Shui purposes more difficult, it can also change your Pah Kwa 'reading' considerably. An irregularity in the shape of the house becomes a protrusion when the area which juts out is less than half the length of the relevant side of the house; it becomes an indentation when the area which juts out is more than half the length of the relevant side of the house.

A protrusion tends to strengthen whatever chi energy is found on that side of the building while an indentation diminishes it, but if the protrusion is, say, 45 per cent of the length of the house, it will often result in an excess of chi – which is negative regardless of favourable direction. If an indentation is very small – say, much less than one-third of the width of the house – it has a minimal effect in terms of this aspect of Feng Shui and can be ignored. For the purposes of this section, a protrusion of excessive proportions can be taken to have similar negative properties to an indentation. Depending on the facing direction of the relevant wall, protrusions and indentations will have very different effects on life for the householders, as summarised below.

North – large protrusions and indentations in the north are generally unfavourable. An indentation here may make the occupants accident prone and has been linked to loss of sexual appetite and fertility problems. While a small protrusion helps create a quieter atmosphere, also promoting fertility, a large extension can lead to isolation.

North East– a protrusion on this side of the house will encourage good health and financial development provided it is not too large, but there is also a risk of instability. A large protrusion can upset the flow of chi throughout the building, however. An indentation indicates lack of motivation and financial loss.

East – a protrusion may encourage the occupants to take unnecessary risks, but if it is small it may be suitable for young people at the starting point of their career. An indentation leads to caution and lack of drive, which in turn leads to business setbacks.

South East – a small protrusion promotes harmonious relationships and is particularly favourable for the marriage prospects of daughters. However, young women may have difficulty finding a partner if there is a indentation here. For businesses, this can translate itself into financial setbacks.

South – a protrusion proportional to the rest of the house indicates that the occupants will be respected and enjoy a full social and public life. However, a large extension can overwhelm the occupants with heightened emotions and a bloated sense of self-importance. Traditionally, an indentation indicates that the daughters of the house will be led astray, or that the family honour will be lost.

South West – when there is a large protrusion in the south west, the women will control the house and the men will let them. This is not as delightful as it might sound, since it also tends to lead to chronic laziness in men! A small protrusion is favourable for family harmony, however, while a deep indentation can bring health problems to the oldest woman in the house.

West – in the west, a protrusion indicates family happiness, financial success and romance, but if it is too large the occupants are likely to become rather self-indulgent. An indentation indicates a tendency towards flirtation and discontent.

North west – a protrusion will encourage a competitive atmosphere and a sense of responsibility, which should bring rewards for the family's security. If it is too large, however, the father could become authoritarian. An indentation will lead to rebellion and quarrels.

This is just a brief guide, but a protrusion or indentation which is on an unfavourable side of the house is not necessarily a disaster for the occupants. For an indentation, the 'missing chi' (i.e. the chi which would be inside the house if the indentation did not exist) can be 'replaced' by lining plants on the outer side of the external wall. The use of mirrors on the inside of an indentation will have the same effect. Using colours and materials to offset the negative effects of a protrusion or indentation is also an effective method.

Roof shapes

The shape of your roof can profoundly influence not only the type and quality of the chi in your own home, but also the fortune of your neighbours. A steep roof with sharp corners or many angles may send arrows of chi into your neighbours' homes – and the steeper the roof the more harmful the arrows will be. This can indirectly affect your own home if your neighbours use Feng Shui cures such as mirrors that deflect the bad fortune back towards you.

Like the main part of the building, roof shapes are linked to the five elements. A steep roof or a pointed turret represents the fire element which is unfavourable, partly for the reasons stated above. Too often, turrets incorporate a number of negative factors which include spiral staircases, which generate sha chi, and elongated or triangular room shapes (*see* Building types, page 204). A shallow pitched roof represents the earth element and thus provides the security necessary for a stable family life. Although gently pitched 'pyramid' roofs are favourable in shape, the association of pyramids with burial and death means they are susceptible to a predominance of yin energy, and are not thus suitable for homes. A roof which reaches very nearly to the ground is thought to cause weakness and ruin, while a flat roof makes for a dull, uneventful life.

Building types

Although many people do not have much choice as to where they live – and this is also true of homeowners, limited as they generally are by location and budget – it is useful to know what to look out for so that some attempt can be made to remedy sha chi, for example. Ordinary houses, whether detached or semi-detached have, to some extent, been mentioned elsewhere and aspects of Feng Shui concerning gardens will be dealt with in a later section. However, in certain buildings, there are additional points to consider.

High rises
Living in a block of flats means there is chi coming into your home that you have no control over, and this may require you to take corrective measures. Si chi may be produced in shared hallways if they are cluttered and dirty, while sha chi can be generated by straight, narrow corridors. Placing a Pah Kwa over the door to your flat as you would the main entrance of a house will protect the occupants to a certain degree. There are also Feng Shui cures you can put in place for poor alignment of doors (*see* Inside Your Home/Doors, page 113). If you are aware of heavy furniture and water placements on the floor above you, these should also be corrected by a few simple adjustments (*see* Interior Decoration/Ceilings, page 185).

Where a block of flats is much taller than the surrounding buildings, it will protrude out of the area's energy field and will be vulnerable to sha chi from the west as well as being over-exposed to the wind. As earlier sections have mentioned, the ideal situation for your home is where it is protected by hills to the north (Assessing Your Building/Symbolic animals, page 99), so it is best to avoid the upper flats in a high rise. Similarly, if the building is the lowest in an area of high rises, its chi will be oppressed and it is important to avoid flats on the lower floors (as well as houses that are located between high rises). In an area where buildings are of similar height, a flat on the middle floor is ideal. A number of high-rise buildings have car parks situated underneath them. While basement car-parks do not present any significant problems, when they are located on the ground level below the building they can create a serious obstacle to the flow of chi to the flats above.

The commonest cause of bad Feng Shui associated with apartment blocks comes from the corners of neighbouring buildings or from wind tunnels between other high rises. This is neutralised if the building has semi-circular balconies, which deflect harmful arrows of chi from these external factors.

Flats above shops

Even a two-storey building can have its complications, particularly if you live over certain retail establishments. It is not difficult to think of shops above which you would be happy or unhappy to live. Compare, for example, an undertaker's premises with a flower shop, or a betting shop with a bank. There are obvious differences and the chi will vary accordingly.

Basement flats

Basement flats are regarded as being contrary to good Feng Shui since they lack natural light, inhibiting the circulation of chi around the home. Entering the home from a dark stairwell is inauspicious, as chi will tend to stagnate here (*see* Inside Your Home/Doors, page 113), while climbing steps to leave your

Figure 76: Front door lower than level of road [bad Feng Shui]

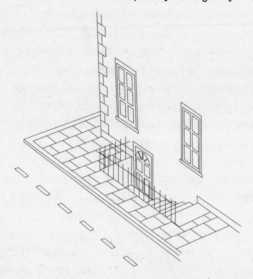

home indicates personal struggle (*see* Figure 76). Flats which are below the level of the land may not benefit from positive chi flowing from positive natural surroundings, and associated problems of damp produce an excess of yin energy. It is not all bad news, however. Many techniques used in interior design to make basement flats more bearable – such as skilful use of glass, chrome, mirrors and light/bright colour schemes – can also do much to address the lack of chi in this type of home. Although open-plan rooms are one way of making the most of natural light, each section should be clearly delineated so that it does not impinge on other areas of work or rest (*see* Inside Your Home/Feng Shui for small houses, page 172).

Loft apartments

There is nothing fundamentally wrong with sleeping on the top floor of a building or in locating a room in the loft space of your house in Feng Shui terms. However, loft-style apartments tend to share a number of common factors which make them undesirable from the Feng Shui point of view.

First of all, the loft apartment is often open plan. As discussed in earlier sections (Inside Your Home/Feng Shui for small houses), it is better for different rooms to be designated to different functions – as the chi that you will need to flow in a room for socialising, for example, will not suit a room allocated to quiet reading or sewing. While there are some simple remedies for separating a dining room from a lounge, it is particularly unfavourable for a kitchen to be combined with a room such as the lounge (*see* Inside Your Home/Feng Shui for small houses). In an open plan flat, the possibility that items of furniture, such as the stove and the bed, might face one another or that the staircase might be opposite the wrong door is much increased. Incompatible combinations of rooms and furniture are discussed in previous sections (*see generally* Inside Your Home, page 111).

The second consideration is that many loft apartments have oversized rooms in which the chi can easily dissipate. A very high roof might mean that a mezzanine floor is included in the overall design, and this has its own implications (*see* Inside Your Home/Feng Shui for small houses). Spiral staircases and stairs with open risers are also a common feature in loft spaces, and can adversely affect the flow of chi (*see* Inside Your Home/The stairs, page 151). Thirdly, a loft apartment is likely to have ceilings which slope, sometimes down to the floor, and exposed beams. A building which imitates the popular loft apartment style is just as likely to use these design features. Both beams and sloping ceilings are unfavourable, and Feng Shui consultants advise clients not to sleep in such a room (*see* Interior Decoration/Ceilings, page 185).

Finally, a genuine loft apartment is likely to be located at the top of an old often industrial building, be it a brewery, a factory or a warehouse. This has implications of its own, as discussed in the section, Unusual Houses, on the next page.

Terraces

For a house in a terrace, it is necessary to consider the chi from outside (front and back, whatever the directions might be) and also the chi from the homes on either side. Without causing too much annoyance to your neighbours, try to find out what furniture and equipment is kept on the other side of adjoining walls, as this may affect the chi in your own home. There are many rules concerning back-to-back furniture – one of the most important is that a stove should not be placed behind the head of a bed. All of these rules are dealt with in the chapter, Inside Your Home, page 111.

In a terraced house it is necessary to consider your position in relation to the other houses in the row from an external point of view. While, in terms of real estate, either end of the terrace might be regarded as the most advantageous, this will be inauspicious if the terrace is situated on a hill – as the house on the lowest ground can be subject to stagnant chi, while the house on the highest ground might suffer from over-exposure

Figure 77: A house on the lowest ground in a terrace [bad Feng Shui]

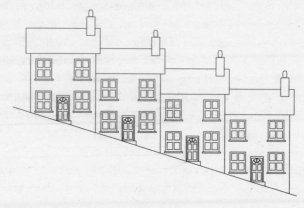

to chi from the west, for instance (*see* Figure 77).

It is significant that houses in a terrace often have a similar internal layout. For example, the front door of each house is usually facing the same direction, the occupants may even sleep facing the same direction, and they will all be subject to the same or similar external factors. This, if the direction, is favourable, can promote communication and harmony in the neighbourhood. However, if the houses are facing a less favourable direction, there could be friction between the various homes as well as general lack of good fortune for the residents.

New-build homes

The layout of modern housing estates is increasingly geared towards the requirements of different families. Thus it is quite easy to find a new-build home to fit your general needs, and if you have had a consultant look at your personal Feng Shui, you may be able to find the house which is most suited to you. However, this might also work against the existence of community as this tends to develop when homes are of a similar layout and facing direction (*see* Terraces, page 208). When homes are laid out around an estate you need to consider the increased possibility of sha chi from your neighbours roofs and gardens, and the shape of the estate or plot itself. An estate which resembles the shape of a kitchen chopper or knife is considered unfavourable, especially if your house is located on the 'blade'. The layout of roads is considered below. One further consideration is that many new homes use natural materials, such as timber frameworks, which is thought to promote positive chi.

Unusual houses

Although Feng Shui and the tenets of real estate often agree, this is not always the case. In particular, properties which boast unusual features too often have chronic Feng Shui problems – as seen in reference to building shapes (*see* page 198). Homes situated in converted churches and railway carriages/stations are much sought after, but as it is not good Feng Shui to live within sight of a church or railway station, it is even less favourable to live inside one. In addition to the overwhelming yin chi of being associated with a house of final rest, a church conversion often has sharp irregular angles and oversized rooms. A railway station is associated with constant movement, noise and pollution. Other inauspicious conversions are barns, schoolhouses, hospitals, warehouses and factories. It is important to trace the history of an old building converted into flats as many causes of excessive yin energy may be unearthed in the process. Renovation, too, can create new problems (*see* Interior Decoration/Renovation, page 179).

Even the only slightly unusual home can be a source of bad Feng Shui. A garage built into the house is desirable from the point of view of convenience, but as an empty room it is a source of negative or dead chi (*see* Figure 78). This also applies to an open car port on the ground floor of the building. The negative chi seeps into any room located above the garage, and can cause particular problems if the bedroom or office is located here. Garages are best built at a distance from the house and

Figure 78: A garage built into the house [bad Feng Shui]

Figure 79: A cantilevered house with a bedroom in the unsupported section [bad Feng Shui]

reached by a curved rather than straight driveway. Houses in which the upper floor is larger than the lower, particularly houses where support is provided by brackets from the lower wall, are also unfavourable (*see* Figure 79). A bedroom or study should not be located in the 'unsupported' section, as this will cause a certain 'lightness' which encourages sleeplessness or lack of concentration.

Houses with turrets or towers will harness negative chi if they have a sharp pointed roof or corners, a spiral staircase, or if they create a triangular shaped room. However, while bedrooms should not be circular, a bathroom situated in a round turret can be beneficial. Irregular-shaped houses and their relationship to the five elements are discussed in the section on building shapes, page 198 (*see also* Yin and Yang/ Significance of the five elements, page 47).

The immediate surroundings

In addition to the physical structure of your house or building, the scope of Feng Shui includes the surrounding area and its effects on the fortunes of your own home and the neighbourhood in general. The man-made features most likely to influence chi in your home are roads and other buildings, while in the natural landscape, trees and water can have a major impact on your fortune.

Roads

The location of your house in relation to nearby roads is worth examining in some detail, as roads are major channels for the flow of chi. Many of the principles governing roads are equally applicable for streams and rivers, which act as conveyers of chi in much the same way. Gentle winding roads are preferable to straight roads with sharp and possibly dangerous bends along which chi is likely to travel too fast. As mentioned at the beginning of Part I, houses located at T-junctions or where a road is curving away from your house (Figure 4) can cause knife-like sha chi. In addition, houses located in cul-de-sacs, facing a Y-shaped road, at a crossroads, or just after a road has forked into two, will all suffer in their fortunes (*see* Figure 80).

At a crossroads, mirrors outside the home will help deflect the sha chi generated by sharp angles and converging traffic. The use of mirrors, fences and

Figure 80: Bad house locations in relation to the road

Outside Your Home

small trees will help address the powerful chi generated by a T-junction. Mirrors can also help deflect the knife-like effect of overpasses and roads which curve away from your house. A cul-de-sac would benefit from a small pathway being cut into it so that the chi does not stagnate at the end of the road.

Conversely, a jumbled network of roads can confuse and trap the chi. Gentle, rounded designs and plenty of green leafy plants outside your home can help offset this negative effect. A site near an overpass is unfavourable as powerful sha chi can be directed towards the home. The worst location in this case would be in the shadow of the overpass or in an apartment parallel with the bulk of the overpass. Screening off the windows with plants and curtains and, if you have a garden, growing a row of shrubs outside will help counteract this (*see* Figure 81). Surprisingly, the traffic roundabout is not necessarily a bad feature to have near your house – provided you are not in the middle of it, where the chi will miss you altogether. Roundabouts actually decelerate the flow of chi in much the same way as they slow traffic, and this is favourable if there are many straight roads – as mentioned above. In an inner-city

Figure 81: An overpass next to a block of flats [bad Feng Shui]

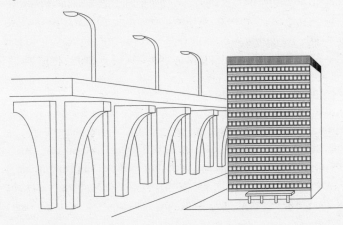

area where parks may be few and far between, a roundabout with a patch of greenery and some bushes can add much-needed sheng chi from the ground.

In terms of convenience, it may seem like a good thing to live a short distance from a bus stop, but according to Feng Shui principles this is bad if you can see it from your home. That is because the bus stop sign is associated with sharp sha chi. Other transport nodes, such as train stations and subway entrances are also unfavourable. A subway will drain away your positive chi, and should be offset by curtains, blinds or shrubs. The power cables and vibration of a nearby railway track are regarded as having a negative influence on the Feng Shui of your home.

As a symbol of communication between two banks of a waterway, as well as a feat of engineering, a bridge near your home can be favourable. However, if many roads converge near the bridge, the chi can simply be too strong for domestic life. In this case, a mirror may help deflect the chi, and blinds and curtains can also be helpful. Businesses may positively thrive where these roads converge, but underneath the bridge it is a very different story. If it arches over your home or business, the indication is that your building has been left behind in the pursuit of progress. Furthermore, traffic and people are literally travelling over your head – resulting in pressure to the chi and possible tension and headaches in your household.

Neighbouring buildings

Surrounding buildings primarily affect your fortune if they direct arrows of sha chi at your home, from sharp corners, gables, chimney pots, aerials, roof angles, and so on. Other pointed objects such as tall trees, a clothes line prop, an electricity pylon, or the frame of a swing, can also generate sha chi if they are pointed at your home. These have all been dealt with in earlier sections (*see* Figures 5 and 6). It is unfavourable if your home is boxed in by other buildings, situated in the gap or 'wind tunnel' between two taller buildings, or in the shadow of a larger building.

While it is not good Feng Shui for your front door to be directly opposite your neighbour's front door, it is also bad to be facing the gap between two buildings. The shape and material of surrounding buildings in relation to your own building shape and material is also relevant (*see* Yin and Yang/ Moderating elemental conflicts, page 55). A house which faces a church, electricity substation, cemetery, hospital, police station, or rubbish tip is in an unfavourable location (*see* Figure 82). If any of these are visible from your windows or front door, you will need to apply the Feng Shui cures outlined in the relevant section (Inside Your Home/Doors/Windows, pages 113 and 124).

Figure 82: A view of a church/substation [bad Feng Shui]

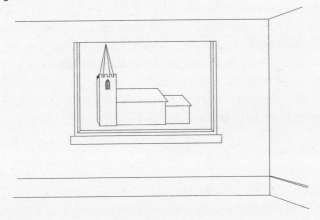

Water

Water is a very useful element to have around us as it has a soothing effect and it also carries chi. It is preferable to have a modest stretch of water – a small stream or pond – rather than a vast lake or a large man-made canal. This is because the best form of chi moves at a modest pace and does not travel in straight lines. This type of chi is associated with streams and smaller bodies of water. Conversely, sha chi travels in straight lines and is more likely to be generated by a canal than a stream. Also, a large body of water may be too oppressive for some as it builds up chi and if it were to your west it may build up sha chi. Also, as mentioned at the outset (*see also* Figure 4) it is not good to have water, such as a river, flowing straight towards your house.

Water is, however, vital and if it is absent outside, then it can be provided indoors through the use of an aquarium, or perhaps a small fountain in a conservatory.

Trees

Trees are also important and they complement the buildings, the latter being considered as the yang element in the immediate surroundings while the trees are the yin element. There has to be a balance between these different aspects and a useful guideline is to have 40% yin and 60% yang in your surroundings. This means that buildings and hills (the yang part) can occupy three fifths while trees and hollows in the land take up two fifths. Trees provide a balancing factor for the buildings and the hills and are clearly, therefore, very important. Further aspects of the use of trees will be considered in the section on Designing Your Garden.

CHECKLIST 10 Outside your home
- Basement flats, loft apartments and unusual conversions are generally regarded as unsuitable homes in Feng Shui.
- A roundabout can actually be a favourable feature near the home, if chi would otherwise flow too fast.

- Roofs should be gently pitched. A steep roof can generate harmful sha chi.
- Too many roads can confuse and trap chi, but a house sited just after the road has forked into two can suffer from a lack of chi.
- It is very inauspicious for a house or business to be located under a bridge.
- Your front door should not face a police station, church, cemetery or hospital.

Location

There is much about Feng Shui that is very obvious and it is quite easy to assess a building and its location. Clearly a house in an industrial centre is not going to be as desirable as a pleasant semi-detached home on a new site next to fields, or a cottage set amongst woods, and so on. Most people will benefit from living in or near to countryside where there is fresh air, attractive views, trees and greenery and perhaps a stream or a lake. It is appreciated that this is not very helpful advice for people who live and work in cities, however. Much depends anyway on the age of the individual person as the city may appeal to the younger generation, at least for a time. While it is often the case that at some point we all would like to have a more peaceful environment, the modern practitioner of Feng Shui must examine the fundamental principles underlying the philosophy and interpret them in tune with life as it is today. It is worth adding one or two specific points about life in three areas – the city, the countryside and the seaside.

Urban
Life in a busy city with noise and vehicle exhaust pollution, possibly run-down buildings and certain inner-city problems

217

Feng Shui

will be subject to much sha chi and a great deal of effort will be necessary to remedy this situation. However, there is much that can be done inside the home to make your own environment as encouraging to the flow of chi as possible. There are also measures that can be taken to deal with external aspects such as roads and other buildings (*see* above). Although, in general, water is a positive conveyor of chi, urban watercourses can be less favourable. Fenced off, diverted in underground tunnels, artificially straightened, and clad in unsightly concrete, the streams and rivers that flow through large towns and cities are often turned from natural channels of sheng chi into drains. They will thus have the same negative effect as an open drain on the Feng Shui of your building. If you live near a degraded watercourse, it is worth putting pressure on the relevant local body or council to improve the situation.

Rural

Although the countryside home is likely to be more beneficial in Feng Shui terms than the city home, this does not mean that external factors are not to be taken into consideration. The distance between houses in the countryside is often too wide for sha chi from the neighbours to be a problem. However, outbuildings, fences, washing lines, and features of the natural environment – such as fast-flowing rivers, high hills to the front or tall trees – can also generate sha chi.

Homes built on a hillside should not be located at the highest point where chi can be excessive, near the edge of a steep hill, or beneath an overhang. The facing direction of the hill is also important, as if you are on a side perpetually in shade you could be subject to an excess of slow-moving yin energy. In addition, rounded hills represent the metal element and are more yin; while steep, jagged mountains represent the fire element and are more yang. The front of a hillside home should overlook lower ground, preferably with a stream or river embracing it, but it is best if the hills behind the house are gentle. If they are too steep, positive chi will roll straight past the house, leaving the occupants bereft of good fortune. Corrective measures, such as trees planted behind the house, will need to be taken (*see* Figure 37).

A house which is too isolated will be vulnerable to excess chi which can be negative, especially if it is exposed to sha chi from the west. If there are no natural hills to protect the house, planting a row of trees on the exposed side will help shield it from fast-moving chi. This would also be helpful if the land is dry and the vegetation sparse, as this kind of environment is likely to produce si chi, or dead chi. The front of the house should not, however, be hidden by trees. A gentle valley is quite acceptable as a location for a house as the surrounding hills protect it from the elements. As valleys are quite yin, plenty of yang surfaces and items in the home may be suitable. A narrow valley with steep sides will oppress the chi and might funnel it too rapidly towards the house. This can be redressed, to some extent, by well-placed trees.

Seaside

Seaside homes should not be located on a promontory or near a cliff-edge, as the over-exposure to the elements of wind and water will make it difficult to accumulate chi. The seaside home will ideally be sited north facing the sea to the south; west facing the sea to the south east; or north east facing the sea to the south west. It should be embraced by hills, with only the ground to the front having wide exposure or a view over an expanse of water.

Designing
Your Garden

It is very easy to concentrate so much upon the interior decor of your house that the garden is ignored; or perhaps you simply can't stand gardening anyway. Applying Feng Shui to the garden introduces a new perspective and one which is both interesting and productive.

As a general principle, and this is hardly surprising, the garden should complement the house. However, there is more to it than this simple generalisation. Houses are, in the main, angular constructions and there are many hard lines and sharp corners to them. The garden provides the opportunity to balance these hard edges with flowing shapes and gentle curved lines. If space permits, paths, flower beds, lawns and ponds can all be used to enhance the Feng Shui of your garden.

It is therefore best to avoid hard outlines in the garden, so the plan shown in Figure 83 is not particularly uplifting. It follows the pattern often seen where lawns are rectangular and they are bounded by strips of flower beds. There is often a symmetry about gardens, with a central path and similar features on either side of the path. In China, the tendency is, where there is space to make it possible, to opt for curved paths, rounded beds and lawns. Also, special features are developed and these may be placed around a corner and half-hidden so that it is a pleasant surprise to come across a new view or area of the garden. This might be a fountain or a garden seat partially enclosed by a trellis and climbing plants, or perhaps an arbour, both of which provide a quiet corner. The scope is really quite considerable. Figure 84 shows one possibility for a rearranged garden based upon the site available in Figure 83.

In the new layout, the major changes involve removing all traces of rectangular, regimented flower beds and lawns. All the components are still there but with more flowing outlines and, in addition, a fountain and pond have been at the end of

223

Figure 83: Garden layout before applying Feng Shui principles, illustrating the regimentation and hard edges

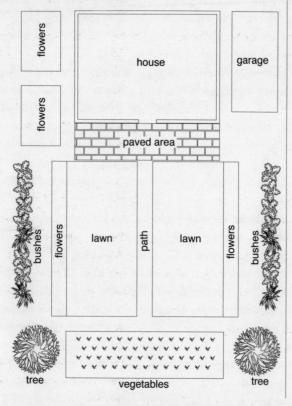

the garden, providing the beneficial effects of water, but also a pleasant scene to be viewed from the garden seat. Next to the house, a paved area is retained but it is softened by use of shrubs in tubs. The placing of a trellis enhances this end of the garden in two ways. It cuts off the back wall of the garage, which is never a pretty sight and it provides a nice enclosed area in which a table and chairs can be sited. This allows a pleasant view of the rest of the garden and it also helps block off any immediate view of the house creating a feeling of

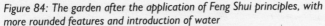

Figure 84: The garden after the application of Feng Shui principles, with more rounded features and introduction of water

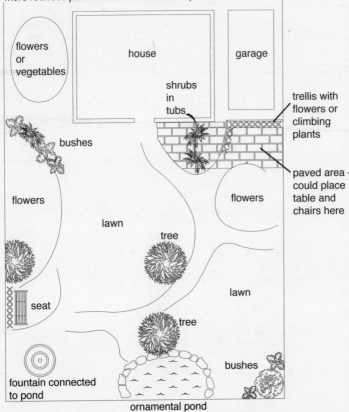

ornamental pond

peacefulness and solitude. This design dispenses almost completely with the small vegetable garden although a bed has been retained next to the house. It would, however, be perfectly feasible to have more ground devoted to vegetables. This could be partially screened from the rest of the garden by a hedge of some description and approached through a flowered arch (using, for example, clematis or honeysuckle). The scope is enormous.

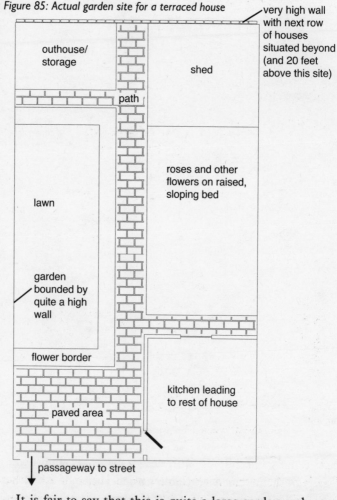

Figure 85: Actual garden site for a terraced house

very high wall with next row of houses situated beyond (and 20 feet above this site)

outhouse/ storage

shed

path

roses and other flowers on raised, sloping bed

lawn

garden bounded by quite a high wall

flower border

kitchen leading to rest of house

paved area

passageway to street

It is fair to say that this is quite a large garden and many modern houses have very much less and some may have just a small yard. Even so, by applying the same principles a great deal can be achieved. Figure 85 shows the garden at the back of a terraced house – the garden is long and thin and is approached from a tunnel-like passage from the street. The

Figure 86: The garden site of Figure 85 modified by applying Feng Shui

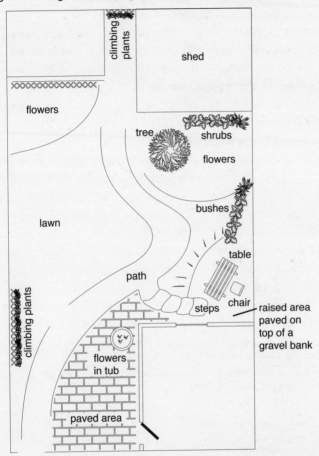

door into the kitchen is effectively the back door of the house. Although the scope in terms of space is limited, much can still be done and Figure 86 shows one possibility. This layout provides a much more inviting scene when entering the garden area from the passage and much more could be done.

Some of the individual features and aspects of the garden are now mentioned beginning with drives and paths.

Drives and garden paths

Many gardens are situated to the front of a house and therefore also contain the main drive and approach to the building. In line with the theme of curved paths and lines in the garden, the same should be applied to a drive. There are many arrangements that adversely affect the flow of chi, for example, straight drives or paths leading directly to the door or a drive narrowing to the door (*see* Figure 87). Sha chi may be generated by a straight drive and chi can be concentrated by a narrowing drive. Too narrow a path will limit the flow of chi. As a general rule, however, a path or drive that has dimensions in keeping with the rest of the house should be fine. Much, of course, depends on the direction from which the chi originates and probably the best direction is south to south-east from which the beneficial yang and sheng chi come (giving a developing and sustaining influence).

In addition, and as stated elsewhere, the drive should not be positioned so that it runs directly up to the door. It is far better to have a curved drive or path, perhaps sloping away gently (*see*

Figure 87: A path running from door to gate. The neighbour's gate and door are also aligned [bad Feng Shui]

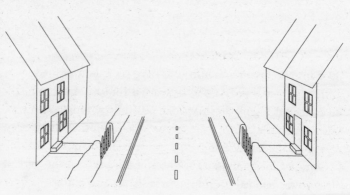

Figure 88. It is better to avoid having the path going alongside the house for any distance as this may result in the chi missing the house altogether.

Figure 88: Preferable configurations for drives/paths to the house

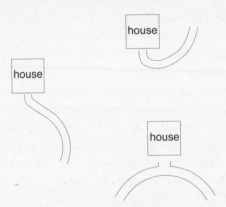

Paths in the garden, whether to the front or rear of the house, should as mentioned be curved to allow the gentle flow of chi. It is also not a good idea if they are totally flat and level – a few small rises and falls will help reduce any sha chi. This is less important if the path or drive runs from the south, but the implication here is that a back garden path running from the south serves a north facing house which itself would need attention!

Trees in the garden

In most cases, it is better to have trees that present a rounded profile which blend in with the rest of the garden. As such, tall spiky conifers and firs are not usually a good idea, unless you live in a very mountainous area. The trees that best fit include willow, maple, magnolia, cherry and similar species.

If you move to a new house where there is a number of

established trees, it is preferable, if at all possible, to leave the older, mature trees where they are. It is not good Feng Shui to chop down such a tree, especially if it is 'protecting' the house in some way and many practitioners take this very seriously indeed. In the 1930s, for example, a small village on one of Hong Kong's outlying islands lost several large trees during a typhoon. When the birth rate of boys in the area subsequently fell, the entire village uprooted, abandoned their homes and moved inland.

The exception to this rule is, of course, when a tree or large shrub is dead or dying, or diseased. In this case it is perfectly acceptable to remove it, and it is recommended that you do so, particularly if the tree or shrub is in the front garden. Roses are also considered by some to be a bad idea as bushes with thorns are not recommended.

Water in the garden

Water is considered to be very important by the Chinese and it is thought to be vital to a garden as it helps the chi to move about and to stay within the garden. That is why many suggestions relating to the layout of gardens will include a fountain and/or a pond, if space permits. Fortunately it is possible to install a fountain in even a small garden at relatively little cost.

Patterns of water flow
In one of the ancient books relating to Feng Shui, the many different configurations that a body of water might adopt, with reference to a building, were listed as an aid in deciding where to build near water. The way in which the water flowed towards or flowed by a building would have significance. One of the ideal situations is to have water in front of your house (*see* Figure 89) which could be a pond. Water flowing towards

Figure 89: The ideal juxtaposition of house and water

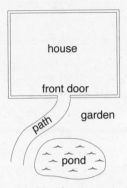

a house can have good and bad effects, depending upon its line of approach. If, as mentioned elsewhere in this book, the water flows directly at the house (*see* Figure 90), then this brings sha chi to the house. If however, the water flows obliquely towards the house (*see* Figure 91), in effect flowing past at an angle, this is quite favourable and is thought to bring financial success.

When the water flows past a house, it takes away the things that are bad and it is considered beneficial if the river or

Figure 90: This location is ill advised

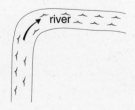

Figure 91: The favourable configuration of water flowing towards, and past, a house

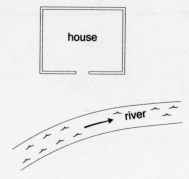

stream is then hidden from view as it leaves the location. Another beneficial arrangement is if the water flows along the front of the house and then turns to the side. There are two variations depending upon direction and orientation (*see* Figures 92 and 93). The opposite, water turning away from a building, is not favourable. A pool in front of a house, which nevertheless is part of a river or stream flowing past in a favourable way, is also very beneficial as it represents the accu-

Figure 92: A beneficial arrangement where the stream or river is said to 'embrace' the house

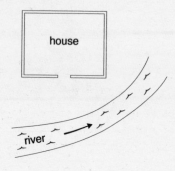

Figure 93: *This arrangement is considered very favourable indeed, as it can confer good luck on the house*

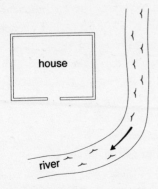

mulation of wealth. Also, because flowing water carries beneficial chi, it is very good for a house to be situated just beyond the point in a river where two tributaries converge to make one flow (*see* Figure 94). This is because the chi from both arms of the river combines and forms an enlarged flow with greater chi. The opposite of this, where the house is situated after a fork in the river, is not so good because the chi of the one river is being divided into two and thereby weakened.

Figure 94: *A highly beneficial situation at the convergence of two streams or rivers*

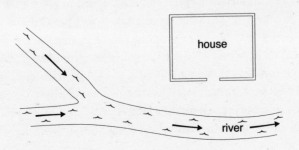

Hedges, shrubs and climbers

Hedges are very useful in gardens to help mark out areas without the use of harsh lines as created by fences or stones. It is also possible to make little corners and quiet areas with the use of hedges although it may take some planning and time to fully achieve your aim. It is preferable to select hedges with a natural look such as beech rather than trimming hedges such as privet to a hard-edged box-like barrier. In keeping with the general principles outlined, hedges should not be set out in straight lines but in gentle curves, if at all possible.

Both trees and climbers can be grown around some sort of framework to make a screen or arbour. Clematis and honeysuckle are particularly good in this respect but any fragrant climbing plant would be suitable. To help camouflage the hard corners of a house it is also possible to train climbers up the walls. This is fine up to a point, but it is important that it is kept under control and that the fabric of the house is not allowed to suffer as a result.

The use of paving stones

Areas covered with paving stones or slabs of some description can look very nice – they can also look rather sterile. It is therefore important to plan carefully where to place this area and precisely how it is to be laid out. It will probably be near the house, or if there are two, one can be nearer the house. In Figure 84 on page 225, a second paved area could be placed at the bottom left of the garden next to the fountain area. This could be surrounded with plants, bushes and climbers on an trellis to create an arbour-like corner.

As with many other aspects of Feng Shui, it is better not to have too regular an arrangement so if square slabs are used (say two-foot square), try to avoid a regular pattern. An offset will help, or if smaller units are used a more intricate arrangement may be possible. Concrete paving stones are now available in many different shapes which can be used to good effect. In addition bricks can be used to create patterns, such as herringbone. Flagstones are ideal for paved areas as they have a natural appearance that blends in well with plants and the outlines of individual flagstones are randomly shaped.

In addition to considering the shape and arrangement of paving stones, other elements to take into account are what plants/shrubs might be used and should they be in pots and tubs or in gaps in the paving. This gives plenty of flexibility and ensures that any sha chi is broken up – it is the plain straight lines that perpetuate sha chi.

In addition, the careful placing of plants that have fragrant flowers will help the flow of chi and hinder the sha chi. The latter will be found where the smell is not so pleasant so it is worth bearing in mind when choosing the location for your dustbin. Ideally, the bin should be partially enclosed to keep it hidden. This can be achieved with an attractive fence and plants, shrubs suitably arranged.

Flowers

Flowers, particularly those with an attractive fragrance, will grace anywhere, whether growing in the garden or indoors in pots. Pleasant fragrances are very important in Feng Shui and those flowers with especially nice smells are ideal. Commonly used for their smell are honeysuckle, lilac, jasmine and buddleia. In addition, certain flowers are good for chi, among them lotus, lavender, sweet peas and lilies.

Symbolic meaning of flowers

The Chinese, and indeed other cultures, attribute significance and meaning to quite a number of flowers – we are all familiar with the symbol of romance and love as represented by the red rose. On a more light-hearted note, mistletoe means kiss me (and other emotions – *see* below). The following list provides examples, by no means exhaustive, of flower meanings.

Flower	Meaning/Representation
Acacia	hidden love
Amaryllis	pride
Anemone	sincerity
Aster	love
Azalea	womanhood, fragile, also 'Look after yourself for me'
Begonia	be careful
Bittersweet	truth
Bluebell	humility
Bunch of dead flowers	rejected love
Camellia	admiration
Candytuft	indifference
Carnation	fascination; also admiration (red), innocence (white), rejection (yellow), I'll never forget you (pink)
Chrysanthemum	love (red) and truth (white)
Crocus	cheerfulness
Cyclamen	farewells
Daffodil	respect, 'You are the one'
Daisy	purity
Dandelion	happiness and devotion

Flower	Meaning/Representation
Forget-me-not	true love
Forsythia	expectation
Freesia	faith
Geranium	stupidity
Gladioli	professing sincerity
Grass	surrender
Heather	admiration, fulfilled wishes (white)
Holly	happiness at home
Hyacinth	jealousy (yellow), regret and contrition (purple), constant (blue)
Hydrangea	insensitive
Iris	hope and trust, promise
Ivy	affection, friendship
Lilac	beauty
Lily	purity (white), gratefulness (yellow)
Lily of the valley	humility
Magnolia	dignity
Marigold	jealousy
Mistletoe	kiss me, overcoming difficulties, affection
Myrtle	love
Narcissus	correctness
Orchid	refinement, beauty
Pansy	happiness
Peony	compassion
Petunia	anger and bitterness
Poppy	oblivion, also consolation (white), success (yellow) and pleasure (red)
Primrose	I need you
Rhododendron	take care

Feng Shui

Flower	Meaning/Representation
Rose	love and romance (red), purity (white), jealousy (yellow), oneness (red and white), love at first sight (without thorns), grieving (dark red)
Snapdragon	deceit
Stock	loving ties
Sweet pea	leaving, thank you
Tulip	good luck, also I love you (red), warm smile (yellow)
Violet	virtue and faithfulness
Wallflower	faithfulness, particularly through bad times

Feng Shui
for Business

Feng Shui can be applied to one's business whether the site is an office in a room at home or a separate building in the city. Much of what has already been described will apply to the office at home, but this topic will be dealt with shortly. Firstly let us consider business premises and their location and the internal arrangements.

The office building

It is often the case that the Chinese will, when deciding where to establish a business, consider the Feng Shui of the building and also wish to know a lot about it. Although in the west we would wish to have our office in as pleasant a location as possible – it's only natural – in China it is particularly important.

It is important that the shop or office is in an area that is busy and where there is good trade. It may also be important that the street is clean and inviting, otherwise passing trade may be deterred. However, it is not only these essentially superficial factors that are considered, but also the history of the site and shop premises. If the shop has changed hands numerous times and few if any businesses have made a success of their tenancy, then it might be wise to think again and find a more inviting location. If on the other hand, the shop is only available for good reasons, then it may present a better prospect. Perhaps someone is moving on because they have made such a success of their venture that despite their happiness with the current location, they must move to larger premises. This sort of location would seem very auspicious and in the eye of the customers, some of the positive aspects of the previous owner would inevitably make them consider the new business favourably and be willing to give it a try. These are all important aspects of the fuller picture. However, the Chinese will take this further in that, for example, they would avoid

Figure 95: Bad office sites

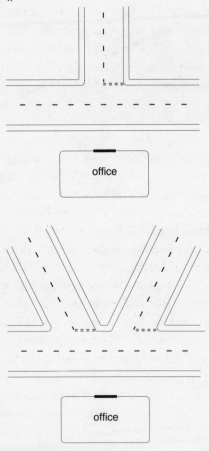

locating a business near to anything that has a connection with death, such as an undertaker's or a graveyard.

The physical location of the building is very important, and the factors that affect houses are also important for offices. For example, there should not be a road or roads aligned opposite the building as this will be a channel for too much chi. The chi moves more quickly than it should and is often called 'killing

chi'. Figure 95 shows bad configurations of roads and buildings while Figure 96 illustrates better layouts. The 'vee'
arrangement in Figure 95 is especially bad because the chi is
directed and funnelled towards your office. In addition to
avoiding roads pointing at your building, it is better not to face
the corner of another building. The sha chi (or secret arrows)
thus generated can be dealt with in many ways including the
placement of mirrors, chimes and so on. However, it may also
be feasible to arrange the shop interior at an angle, so that
instead of following the four walls, the display of goods cuts
across the corners. This has the further benefit of encouraging
the customers to wander around the shop, in contrast to the
'four-cornered approach' (i.e. following the essentially square
or rectangular shape as defined by the building) where corners
can become problem areas which get cluttered and contribute
to the poor flow of chi.

The result and natural response to being faced with this
negative chi is to be defensive and protective which is probably not a good emotion to have when it comes to business and
the job of communicating and selling. The ideal sites in Figure
96 have the road aligned across the front of the building and if

Figure 96: Good office sites

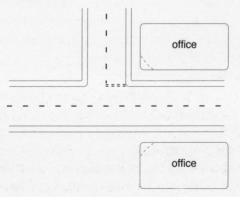

the door is at the corner (as indicated by the broken line) of the building, then so much the better. This idea developed from the practice mentioned above of laying out the shop interior at an angle to the building. If a building has a poor location and orientation, moving the position of the door affects the whole Feng Shui analysis, in effect, altering the position of the building itself. This arrangement was adopted a great deal, and still is, because it is generally considered that putting the doorway across the corner of a building is good Feng Shui practice. In some businesses, the door can be set at an angle and also set back allowing display windows to be placed alongside the extended entrance enabling customers to browse.

Once someone has stepped over the threshold to go inside an office building, the reception area is where most people gain their initial impression of the company. So, even if the building itself is not in an ideal location, much can be achieved inside and particularly in the entrance. Mirrors can be used to a certain extent to reflect bad chi and chimes or similar hanging items may be useful. A welcoming and positive area with good Feng Shui can be created by the use of screens, plants, and perhaps even a fountain. This can block a less than interesting view outside, which in many cases may be urban sprawl or industrial sites. This aspect also links to the five elements, because the introduction of screens and plants represents wood, a fountain or pond is water, red fish in an aquarium fire and water, and stones around the fountain or pond are earth. In this way, the moderating influences can be introduced, in unison with the layout of rooms also recommended for good Feng Shui.

Applying the five elements

Bringing together all the information regarding the five elements, this can be used to assess an office and its immediate

244

location to try to ensure that it is best suited to the business to be carried out there. The element of the location itself must be determined by taking account of, in particular, the direction of facing, and also the surrounding area. In many cases the office will be situated in a city and therefore we should look at the surrounding buildings. Are there a lot of tower blocks, steep roofs, arched buildings, and so on? This will give an indication of the element of the location that can then be assesses against the element of the building.

When this has been established, the five elements can be studied in relation to the business activity to be undertaken and the product coming out of the business. The important factor here is to have the element that most closely matches the business activity through the element produced. That is, if wood is likely to be the best element, then water is a good element because that generates wood in the cycle. If the element of the building does not match the element required, then this is when the use of moderating elements becomes very important.

In the office

There are two basic elements to most office buildings – the offices themselves, the rooms where everyone works, and the corridors connecting them all. Many buildings layouts are now open-plan but most will have some rooms with joining corridors.

The guidelines and suggestions made about corridors with reference to the home apply equally well here (*see* Inside Your Home/Internal doors, page 123). In essence, the points to remember are that too many doors in a corridor or hallway can lead to confusion and, ideally, doors should be placed at regular intervals. Doors should not overlap each other a little as this indicates antagonism and probably the best arrangement, if a

Figure 97: Positioning a desk within an office; good positioning (top) and bad positioning (bottom)

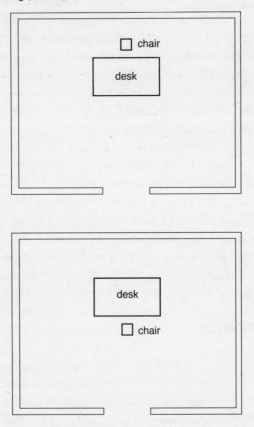

number of doors are necessary, is to have them regularly spaced (*refer back to* Figure 41a and b on page 122). Mirrors or plants can be used to good effect where this ideal arrangement is not possible (*see* Figure 41c). In addition, the immediate area can be improved through the use of suitable lighting and internal decor.

Once inside an office, it is important that the desk or desks be placed in their optimum position. Many people spend a great deal of time sat at a desk and consequently, adequate thought should be given to its position in the office space. The position to avoid is with the desk and chair placed such that you are forced to sit with your back to the door. Figure 97 indicates the desk and chair in good and bad positions. The good position is a parallel of the honoured-guest position in a home where sitting in this chair allows a complete overview of the room, to see everything that is happening and to see any-one entering the room. Another possibility is to place the desk diagonally across a corner of the room but still allowing full vision of the door. If there are two desks in this office, then the diagonal configuration is ideal (*see* Figure 98) as it allows both occupants to have a good position with respect to the door and each other, i.e. they are not forced to sit opposite each other, in a more confrontational set up. This is an interesting develop-ment because placing the desks in this way begins to conform to the shape of the Pah Kwa.

Ideally a desk should not be placed so that it is in a direct line to the door; it is important to be facing the door but at an angle, as indicated in Figure 98. Also, the desk should neither face or back directly on to a window. Other options for placing

Figure 98

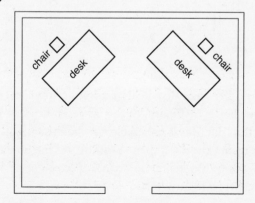

Figure 99: Further options for placing a desk in an office

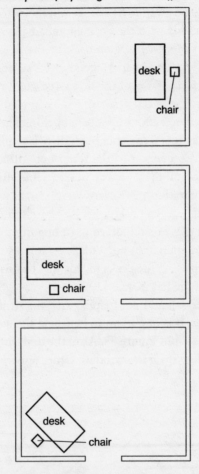

the desk, other than diagonally across the top corner of the room are shown in Figure 99 and in each the desk is at an angle to the door. If it is preferable for whatever reason to have the desk facing the door, then it will help if the direct line to the door can be blocked by some sort of screen or perhaps filing cabinets (*see* Figure 100).

Figure 100: Remedial action to be taken if the desk is facing the door

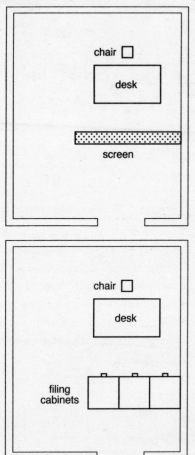

In some offices, there are a number of desks to be accommodated, whether it is the open-plan type of office or what used to be called the typing pool. In either case it is important that the arrangement of desks is such that there are as few straight lines as possible. The configuration should not create channels along which the chi flows too quickly; in all cases

Figure 101: Bad location of desks

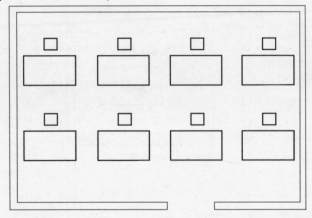

remember the need to create flowing lines for the gentle circulation of chi. Figures 101 and 102 indicate the bad and good location of desks respectively, in this situation. The optimum octagonal Pah Kwa shape can be attempted as shown in Figure 102, but the position of the door does hinder this somewhat. Remember also that this is only a diagrammatic representation and an office with eight desks, with associated office furniture

Figure 102: Good location of desks

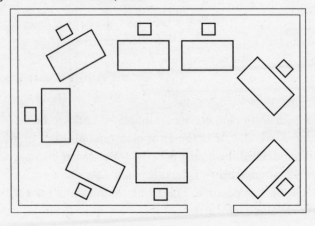

would inevitably be larger than that drawn here! However, it does indicate the sort of layout that should be attempted. If, for any reason, and particularly in an office containing a single desk, it is not possible to have a set-up where the desk faces the door, then a remedy is to place a mirror on the wall that the desk faces. At least then the occupant can see who is entering the room.

An open plan office can sometimes occupy the whole floor of a building and contain twenty or thirty desks. In this case it is not sensible or possible to configure the space as one office and therefore screens are used to create corridors and small office-like areas. The same principles apply and within each screened-off area, the desk can be paced in the best position. The use of such screens does have the added benefit of allowing plants to be trailed over corners, pictures and mirrors to be placed strategically and pathways/corridors and entrances to areas to be positioned correctly.

Many people now work from home, combining the demands of running a business with the needs of a family. It is therefore often necessary to use, as an office, a room that also doubles as, for example, a lounge. As discussed in a previous section, there are a number of aspects to consider which would be applied to an office but which may be affected by being in the home environment (*see* Inside Your Home/Other rooms/The home office, pages 166, 167). The office should obviously be propitious to work, but at the same time be peaceful. This can often be difficult, particularly if there are other people in the room, and especially if they are children! This can to some extent be dealt with by the creation of an office space through the use of screens or, as shown above, by the strategic placing of filing cabinets or bookshelves. This shows it is a different area, with a different function and yet it is not totally cut off from everything else.

The office should not be too cramped, nor need it be too roomy, and a rectangular area is probably best. The feeling generated in the room should lead to clarity of thought, another good reason for partially delineating the office area in another room. If the view out of the window is not very pleasant, then curtains or plants should be placed over the window to help stop the sha chi. The centre of the room should be kept clear so the other items of office furniture – chairs, filing cabinets, bookshelves and so on – have to be placed around the edge of the room, although preferably not simply stood against the walls. The same principles apply here as elsewhere in Feng Shui, the most auspicious arrangement is that which mirrors the Pah Kwa, thus some items – for example, the bookshelves – could be placed across a corner.

When deciding upon the layout of the room, the eight-point method can be used (*see* Figure 30 on page 104 and associated text). By placing the points upon the room plan, it is possible to determine the more auspicious positions for the furniture, but particularly the desk. Of course, an office is not used solely for business, commerce etc. in the strictest sense. It may also be where a designer works, or an illustrator, or an author. The position of the desk may therefore be important. The following provides a guide:

For	Place the desk at
business, finance, commerce and related	money, eminence, wisdom, career, friends
artistic and literary activities related to children (books, games, etc.)	wisdom, eminence, pursuits, friends children
social pursuits	marriage, friends, children, family

When the desk has been placed, then the remaining items can follow. These should be positioned carefully so that the room is tidy and uncluttered. All the items in the room – files, books and so on – should be readily accessible. The centre of the room should always be clear if at all possible and it is a good idea to place a rug at the centre. This can provide a point upon which to focus. The closer the colour of the rug is to a representation of water, the better, because deep water is considered helpful in this respect.

CHECKLIST 11 Feng Shui for business
- Office buildings should not be located opposite a fork in the road or a T-junction.
- Doors in the corridor should not overlap with opposite doors as this indicates antagonism in the workplace.
- The desk should not be located so that you have to sit with your back to the door.
- An ideal location for the desk is across a corner, looking into the room.
- In an open plan office, desks should not be placed in rows as this can encourage chi to flow too fast.

Aspects of Life

The motivating force behind the practice of Feng Shui is the desire to enhance or maintain the areas of life that are important to us. These are likely to include health, career, money and relationships – though the degree of importance we attach to the respective areas will depend on each individual's character, background and circumstances.

It should be clear from previous sections in this book that the presence of si chi and sha chi in and around the home or office can eventually lead to bad fortune in all aspects of life. In addition, certain activities when conducted in certain areas of the home will bring more success than if they had been carried out elsewhere. The colours and objects you choose to surround yourself with will also influence your fortunes and, when placed favourably, they can bring very specific rewards in the form of, say, romance or money.

Although ways of improving your fortune have been mentioned in passing in the relevant sections, it is worth taking the time to look specifically at those areas you would like to promote, particularly if you feel they have been suffering in any respect.

Feng Shui for health

If you have a cold you just cannot seem to shake off or you've suddenly become accident prone, the first thing a Feng Shui consultant will ask you is whether you have recently redecorated or moved home. If you have, the chances are that you have somehow disturbed the harmony of your environment, and the consultant will set about trying to find the source of the disturbance. Even without the benefit of an expert, it is not difficult to trace the potential sources of ill-health.

In Feng Shui it is believed that a major cause of health problems is the presence of cutting chi in or around your home, and you should ensure that there are no secret arrows of chi directed at you from external or internal objects. What you need to look out for is any sharp, straight object pointed towards your home, or any sharp corners or items of furniture inside the home. If you never suffered any ill-effects before redecorating, it is very possible that you have removed an object that, unknown to you, was deflecting the chi. Such an object is most likely to be a mirror, but could also be a shiny surface, a white object, or a plant. Make sure you have not moved your furniture so that sharp corners are protruding or that previously hidden problem areas have become visible.

Further points to note with regard to decoration is that you should not move your bed before consulting the Pah Kwa, as well as the general principles governing bedrooms, as outlined in this book (Inside Your Home/The bedroom, page 154). Exposed beams over your bed, dining table or sofa, artwork which depicts grotesque or distorted body parts, and symbols of war, especially guns and antique swords that might have been used in battle, are all potential sources of sickness, according to the philosophy of Feng Shui.

Another major cause of ill-health in the home is an excess of yin chi from water. Thus, as already mentioned elsewhere in the book, you should avoid the following:

- a bed or dining table situated under a water placement
- a bathroom door which opens towards your bed
- a toilet door which opens into the kitchen
- a bathroom in the north of the house
- a septic tank inside the house or in front of the door
- a drain outside your front door (*see* Figure 103).

For a drain outside the main entrance, you should place a potted plant either side of the door. If the bathroom leads into

Figure 103: Draining away good health [bad Feng Shui]

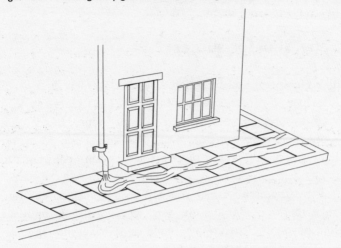

the bedroom or kitchen, you should fit an automatic closer to the toilet door and situate plants and a bowl of salt inside the bathroom. A well or pond which has been left to stagnate or filled up with rubbish causes a huge excess of water chi and, if buried under the house, an old well could cause yin chi to permeate the house, causing illness. To remedy this problem, the well should be filled in professionally. If it is located in the garden, a more straightforward method is to remove as much of the rubbish or dirt as possible, then sink a hollow piece of pipe or bamboo into the area. The hole should be filled with fresh earth, and plants grown around the pipe, which should be protruding by about one foot. It could take more than six months for the yin chi to dissipate.

As well as being aware of the location of all water routes and outlets in and around your home, you should make sure your house is plumbed properly and that this is well-maintained. In Feng Shui, it is believed that dripping faucets and leaking roofs lead to corresponding ailments such as a constant runny

Feng Shui

nose, while clogged pipes and drains are thought to cause blockages in your digestive system.

Feng Shui for success

The placement and direction of your workspace is a major influence in career success. Many of these factors are dealt with in previous sections (*see* Inside Your Home/Other rooms/The home office, page 167 and Feng Shui for Business, page 239) but there are some additional points to remember.

For a successful career you will need a working environment that is predominantly yang, which will help motivate you, but too much yang chi could cause headaches and tension. Thus, you should balance the excessive yang energy of computers and electrical equipment with yin colour schemes, understated lighting, and plants. Avoid L-shaped desks and

Figure 104: Open bookshelves create cutting chi [bad Feng Shui]

open bookshelves which act like blades, directing sha chi across the room (Figure 104).

It is not only your workspace you need to take care of when trying to improve your career prospects. In the bedroom, if you sleep facing the toilet, the chi will be too yin, weakening your yang energy. If you sleep with your head pointing towards the door, your career will stagnate; if, on the other hand, you sleep with your back to the door you are, in effect, allowing people to conspire against you. In Feng Shui, the north is generally associated with progress and development. Therefore, your toilet should not be in the north of your house or it will flush away your career prospects. Plants should not be placed in the career corner of a room as they belong to the wood element which exhausts the water element of the north. Items, such as crystals, that represent the earth should not be placed in this sector either. The best items to place in the career corner would be made of gold or metal, as this generates water and enhances your career prospects.

Feng Shui for money

As with health, the unfavourable placement of water in your home can have unhappy consequences for your finances. If you have a dripping tap, you might find money trickling away, while if you have a toilet in your money corner you are, in effect, flushing away your chances of future wealth. Leaks around the home represent a loss or waste of money while blocked drains can result in delayed payment and a static career. To prevent wealth being depleted you should take care to avoid:

- a water placement at the centre of house
- an open atrium at the centre of the house
- a stove situated with a water placement on the floor directly above

- a water placement over your bed or dining table
- a water tank or bathroom in the north of your house
- a toilet facing the front entrance
- a septic tank inside the house or in front of the door
- a sewage or drainage line under your front door
- a drain outside your front door
- a view of a drain, creek or river with the current moving away from your house, especially if you can see this from your door.

For problem features related to your entrance, you should situate potted plants on both sides of the door. Use plants, salt and an automatic closer to correct an ill-placed bathroom door. Large plants should be grown around an outside water tank. In addition to the cures applied to unfortunate positions, there are also objects you can use to enhance your existing financial prospects. These should be placed in the money area of your home, and in the wealth sector of a room. Appropriate items are metallic or gold in colour. Feng Shui practitioners often recommend the use of antique coins. In China these have square holes at the centre, and are tied together with red thread, then attached to accounts books to attract wealth.

In business, the accounts office or cash register should be placed in the money part of the building, while at home you might want to keep your box of loose change here. Conversely, placing a moneybox near a door or on a window ledge will deplete your funds. Money cats and money frogs placed near the front door are believed to increase the owner's wealth (*see* Interior Decoration/Household accessories/Animals, page 191), and as water represents money, aquariums are often used to activate the money sector of the home (*see* Figure 105). A stream flowing past the house could bring with it good fortune, provided it is in full view of the front door and seems to

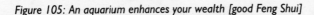

Figure 105: An aquarium enhances your wealth [good Feng Shui]

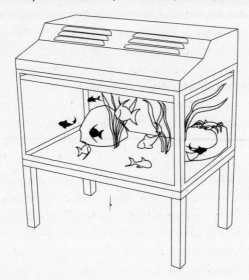

be embracing rather than moving away from you (*see* Figures 92, 93). But a stream flowing behind the house symbolises missed opportunities.

Fishing for fortune

Fortune frogs are a popular accessory in the pursuit of wealth in Hong Kong, Taiwan, Malaysia and other countries and cities where Feng Shui is widely practised. Placed near the main entrance to a building and facing the road, it is believed that they will 'catch' the money of passers-by – which, on a busy street, could be very lucrative indeed! A fortune frog is a rather ugly toad-like ornament with a string of coins around its feet and another coin balanced on its tongue. It is sometimes placed near a cash register in a shop, but always facing the door.

Money cats, originating from Japan, are also believed to

enhance their owners' financial prospects. These cats are often white with gold and black spots (which are meant to represent coins), and are again placed facing the outside door of homes, restaurants and shops.

Feng Shui for love

The theories of traditional Feng Shui with regard to marriage and love are closely linked to the ancient Chinese practice of concubinary whereby a man would have multiple wives and mistresses. The Feng Shui principles were codified from the perspective of the 'number one', or first, wife who would expect to have many more rights than the other wives and mistresses. Clearly, some of the principles governing marriage have no modern application, but it is still possible for both men and women to encourage favourable Feng Shui in order to maintain, improve and repair their relationships. Single people can also do much to attract romance.

In the endowment method, the family corner is represented by the north east while harmonious relationships are represented by the north, and understanding by the east. Each room also has a marriage corner, according to the eight point method, usually the far right hand side of the room as you face inward from the doorway. It is this area upon which you should concentrate if you wish to enhance your love life. Where the marriage area is missing because of an irregularity in the shape of the room or house, it can be extended by the artful placement of a mirror. It will be damaging to your love life if the toilet, kitchen or a storeroom is located in the marriage or family area of the home. You should try not to use a toilet in this area, and should avoid storing mops or brooms here as these items symbolise the sweeping away of romantic opportunity.

To activate romance, both couples and single people may place symbols of marital happiness in the marriage corner of the house or room. Some examples are quartz crystals, the Chinese Double Happiness symbol, a pair of mandarin ducks or love birds in pairs, your wedding bouquet, or your wedding photograph (provided it includes both bride and groom). One pair of items is sufficient – too many could lead to serial relationships! In China, red is the colour traditionally associated with weddings and, indeed, the colour of the 'bridal gown'. It is also, in Feng Shui, the symbol of fire and thus passion. Red roses, a lamp with a red bulb, and even paintings with a splash of red are favourable items to place in the marriage corner.

The bedroom is regarded by Feng Shui practitioners as the essence of the marital home, with the kitchen traditionally seen as coming a close second. If your bedroom is located in the marriage sector of your home, it is a very good sign, but even without this advantage, the use of red or other symbols of

Figure 106: A bed between two doors [bad Feng Shui]

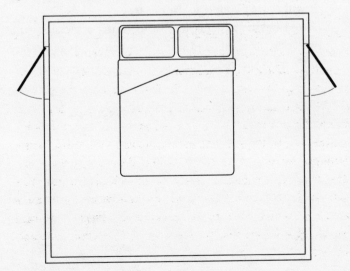

marriage should be sufficient to keep the flame burning. Many of the rules governing the bed have been discussed in previous sections (*see* Inside Your Home/The bedroom, page 154) and general Feng Shui principles should prevail when they conflict with attempts to enhance your love life. The most important rules which affect relationships are as follows:

- The bed should not be placed between two doors (*see* Figure 106). If you cannot move your bed, place a screen between one door and the bed, and an automatic closer on the other.
- Avoid the use of mirrors in the bedroom. When they reflect the couple together, they suggest tension and even the interference of third parties. If a mirror is necessary, it is best kept inside a wardrobe or in an attached dressing room.
- The bedroom should not be situated above a garage or on the 'unsupported' section of a cantilevered floor
- A beam should not run the length of the bed overhead as it will cause a couple to drift apart
- Avoid having an aquarium or anything associated with water on the right hand side of the main door (as you face out), or in the bedroom.

Final
Assessment
Procedures

Although this book certainly does not offer an exhaustive account of Feng Shui, it should allow you to survey your own office or house or to assess a potential new home with confidence. This chapter summarises the various aspects outlined in previous sections in order to help you with your preliminary observations before you embark on a more detailed assessment using the Pah Kwa (Assessing Your Building/Preparation and tools, page 107) and, if necessary, applying the appropriate cures (Feng Shui Cures, page 81). As sometimes practising Feng Shui can be less than straightforward, we have included a brief guide to assessing whether your Feng Shui cures are working. This chapter also incudes a section for the prospective homeowner which, however, is essential reading for anyone keen to make Feng Shui an ongoing part of their life.

Knowing what to look for

In assessing the Feng Shui of your home, the first thing to decide is in which direction it faces and, whilst outside, to assess the approach in terms of roads, paths to the front door and all surroundings features, both natural and manmade. These will include:

Natural
- hills and mountains
- rock slopes
- trees, whether standing alone or in groups
- water in whatever form – streams, rivers, lakes, shores, waterfalls etc.
- valleys, stream beds, fault lines.

Man-made

- roads, tunnels and bridges
- railways
- canals and reservoirs
- cuttings
- electricity cables and wires, electricity pylons, gas tanks, etc.
- a variety of posts, poles and similar items
- fields, hedges and other features created in farming
- residential buildings – houses, flats, cottages, etc.
- public buildings – schools, hospitals, libraries, churches, halls, theatres and cinemas, etc.
- industrial buildings – factories, offices, warehouses, etc.
- commercial buildings – shops, markets, etc.

As already mentioned, some of these features are more likely to affect a building in an urban situation, especially features such as corners, roofs, pipes and posts, and nearby buildings (*see* Outside Your Home/The immediate surroundings, page 211).

It will be possible to make a very quick and reasonably accurate assessment upon arrival at a prospective new home, simply by walking around and being observant. In particular, any features that may generate sha chi should be noted and remedial action considered.

It may also be possible to determine the position of the symbolic animals, the phoenix, dragon, tortoise and tiger. Hopefully at least one can be identified, but this may be easier if considering a house in a rural location, rather than a city office. When considering a house, assess the neighbouring buildings especially if it is a terrace or a semi-detached building. The shared wall or walls will clearly act as a barrier to any external Feng

Shui influences, whether the influence is bad or good.

At the main door, face out, checking the outlook, but also taking account of the path and/or drive approach to the building. As advised previously, it is not a good idea to have a direct approach to the house and any path or drive should ideally follow a curve, as shown in Figure 88. Then look to the main door – it should open inwards to facilitate the inflow of beneficial chi. In the entrance hall note the orientation of the stairs with respect to the door and ensure that the back door is not visible from the front. Both these situations would have to be remedied, as described elsewhere, before the Feng Shui of this building would be acceptable.

When walking around inspecting the rooms, there are a number of general points to bear in mind. Ideally, no window should be directly opposite a door as this may lead to favourable chi leaving the room before it has had time to circulate. This can be overcome in several ways as mentioned throughout the text. Windows facing each other is not an ideal configuration but again this can be remedied. When looking out of the windows, note the surroundings. Are there negative features such as poles, posts, or the corners of a building that may generate sha chi? If so, countermeasures such as the hanging of curtains or the strategic placement of plants, and so on, will have to be adopted. Also, you may be able to see in the landscape one of the symbolic animals, such as the Green Dragon, and this should be complemented by the arrangement of furnishings and the decor. The way in which the chi flows around each room is important – ensure that it will not escape too soon and that it has a suitable entrance and exit.

These basic principles apply to every room in the house. In each case, the flow of chi, the facing directions of the windows and the surroundings immediately outside should all to be taken into account. By referring back to the rooms dealt with earlier, it will be possible to see what should be avoided or what remedial measures may prove necessary. By overlaying the Pah Kwa on the floor plan, the rooms can be better planned.

In the lounge, the windows should ideally face south or west, preferably with a pleasant view. It should be possible to place your furniture to procure the honoured-guest position and if the shape of the room makes such a layout difficult, then the judicious placing of mirrors should permit this. Ensure all chairs can be placed so that they do not back onto a door or window. If the room is an awkward shape, perhaps an exaggerated L shape or a very elongated rectangle, it may be beneficial to screen off part of the room for a related purpose, perhaps for use as a study. Much the same applies to the dining room, except it should be added that some practitioners advocate the dining room windows facing a different direction to the room itself. This helps the favourable flow of chi. The kitchen has been dealt with extensively already, but it is helpful, in addition to following the guidelines provided, to consider carefully the use of the five elements. There are many potential problems in the kitchen with fire, water and sharp kitchen implements, not to mention electric gadgets. Careful planning and use of the elements will help moderate two conflicting elements.

There is little to add about the bathroom except that it is considered good Feng Shui that any water leaving the room should do so in a hidden manner. This mirrors the example of a stream or river flowing past a house into a tunnel or into the ground. In the case of the bathroom, this means that all outlets should be hidden from view. In bedrooms, ensure beds do not face the door. An east or west facing bedroom is ideal.

As you walk around the house, you will build up a picture of the overall Feng Shui of the place, both outside and inside.

In most cases it will prove necessary to make some alterations and additions to improve the Feng Shui – it is unlikely to be ideal. However, you will be able to gauge whether, if thinking of buying, you really want the house from a Feng Shui perspective.

Moving to a new home

In Feng Shui it is believed that sha chi and si chi from previous occupants and events can continue to exist for a considerable length of time. Thus, before moving into a new home there are certain procedures that you should follow to replenish the sheng chi. This is particularly important when a house has been lying empty for some time, since the chi will tend to stagnate. The same techniques should be applied if you have been away from home for a few weeks or if a room has recently been occupied by a sick person. In addition, these techniques, commonly known as 'space clearing', should be applied at least once a year, in order to refresh the chi in your home. Space clearing is conducted along very similar lines to spring cleaning, but there are some important differences.

Stale energy can be replenished by throwing open the windows and doors, as well as cupboards, as soon as you enter your new home. After the initial purge, windows should be opened only two at a time to avoid chi entering and exiting too quickly (*see* Inside Your Home/Windows, page 124). Even if it seems the former occupants have left the house tidy, your new home should be cleaned and aired thoroughly, and any curtains and carpets washed immediately – as dust will lead to an excess of yin chi. It is important that this is done by you or others moving into the house. Feng Shui consultants generally advise clients to sleep in the new home on the day of moving.

Feng Shui consultants generally advise clients only to move

home on certain auspicious days. In addition, the best time to invigorate a new home is after dawn in summer, or in winter – when the sun is at its strongest later in the day – late morning or early afternoon. You should try to avoid clearing space on a cloudy or rainy day; and cleaning should never be done once the sun has set.

Space clearing is often conducted in conjunction with space purifying to purge a house of the influence of previous occupants. One very simple way of purifying the chi in your new surroundings is through the use of fragrance. The type of incense you burn is not important, but it is preferable that it should burn itself out, and be thrown onto earth, not in the bin (Figure 107). Another easy way to wake chi in a house that has been empty, is to walk from room to room with harmonious sounding bells or a metal wind chime. In traditional Feng Shui practice, homebuyers often place an aquarium beside the front door on moving to a new house. Fish, it is believed, will absorb negative energy from the former occupants.

Figure 107

Clearing rituals

In towns and cities with a large Chinese population, loud and colourful rituals for the opening of a new shop or launch of a new business are a common sight. There are a number of traditional Feng Shui rituals which are practised before entering a home for the first time or setting up a new company. These are often performed by a Feng Shui master, but they may easily be carried out at home yourself.

One of the popular methods of space clearing is to sprinkle salt and uncooked rice inside and outside the building, leaving it on the ground until the following morning. First, it is necessary to circumambulate the exterior walls in a clockwise direction, sprinkling the salt and rice at the same time; then repeat the process through every room in the house. A symbolic pagoda held in the left hand is often used in conjunction with the salt and rice to ward off wandering spirits, and a small circular mirror is used to reflect the walls – in particular, dark corners, kitchens and toilets. A Feng Shui master will often carry incense from room to room, waving it in a circular motion while chanting a mantra.

Noise is, of course, a very effective way of dispersing negative chi. Cymbals and sometimes bells are clashed or rung at entrances and corners to scare off negative energies. Firecrackers, used at Chinese New Year and in launching new businesses, work to similar – but much louder – effect.

Self-assessment

When you have assessed your building and installed your Feng Shui cures or corrective measures, small improvements should start to appear in your life and the general atmosphere of the building. Be mindful of any changes that have taken place in your life since starting to practise Feng Shui – if necessary, keep a record, then if things seem to become worse you will be able to trace the source.

An improperly applied cure can of course make matters worse, but if you are sure that the measures you have taken are correct, you should not be too hasty in removing them just because life *seems* to be getting worse. Sometimes an event or situation that seemed a catastrophe turns out to be a remarkable improvement in your life if only you would be patient. Occasionally, however, the chi of a building may still be suffering from negative influences in the past. For this reason, Feng Shui practitioners often conduct space-clearing procedures before they move to a new home. Another reason for continued misfortune might be a source of sha chi or si chi of which you are not aware, such as a badly filled well under your house. The more you know about your building, the easier it will be to deal with any unfavourable situations.

The best thing about Feng Shui is that a significant amount can be achieved quite quickly and with just a little effort. By implementing the procedures outlined in this book, you should be able to make your home or office a better, more comfortable place in which to be.

Glossary

Chen — thunder; one of the eight trigrams that form the Pah Kwa.

chi — the life force, sometimes translated as 'cosmic breath', which is central to the practice and philosophy of Feng Shui. Chi is thought to encompass everything in life.

Chi'en — heaven; one of the eight trigrams that form the Pah Kwa.

five elements — wood, metal, fire, water and earth; the presence or absence of each element is thought to affect the Feng Shui of a building or a landscape.

H'sun – wind; one of the eight trigrams that form the Pah Kwa.

I Ching — the *Book of Changes*.

K'an — water; one of the eight trigrams that form the Pah Kwa.

Ken — mountain; one of the eight trigrams that form the Pah Kwa.

K'un — earth; one of the eight trigrams that form the Pah Kwa.

Li — fire; one of the eight trigrams that form the Pah Kwa.

Lo Shu — known as the magic square, generated when the Pah Kwa is drawn out until the lines impinge upon a square. The magic square is used by Feng Shui practitioners to check, for example, a building's direction and placement.

Luo Pan — a compass with Chinese characters in concentric circles, used in analysing the Feng Shui of a site.

Pah Kwa — (also known as Ba Gua; sometimes known as the Former Heaven Sequence); the octagonal symbol made up of the eight trigrams of the I-Ching and used to assess the Feng Shui of a building and to protect a house from harm.

sha chi — literally translates as 'killing breath'; harmful energy which originates from negative surroundings.

sheng chi — often translated as 'auspicious breath', this is associated with upward movement, and can be found in places that are bright and refreshing.

si chi — the opposite of 'sheng chi'; an energy that is reducing, lessening or dying as a result of a location that is disorderly and decayed.

T'ai ch'i — the well-known symbol for yin and yang, not to be confused with T'ai chi chu'an, the system of exercise.

Tao (or Dao) — 'the way'; a philosophical concept which describes the source of all creation.

Taoism — a religious and philosophical system, also known as 'the way', which was established in China more than 3,000 years ago, and emphasised the importance of nature in dictating the laws of man.

Tao-te Ching — the book written by the philosopher Laotzu, the definitive guide to the union of Heaven and man.

trigram — there are eight trigrams used in I Ching and Feng Shui, each relating to a different natural process under the headings earth, heaven, fire, water, thunder, marsh, mountain or wind.

Tui — marsh; one of the eight trigrams which form the Pah Kwa.

yang — equated with sky or heaven, and balanced with yin. Qualities traditionally ascribed to yang are the active, the positive and the masculine. Yang may be applied to character, occupation, and environment.

yin — equated with earth or creation, and inextricably linked with yang. Qualities traditionally ascribed to yin are the restful, the negative, and the feminine. Yin may be applied to character, occupation and environment.

yin-yang — the Taoist theory that unites opposites, providing balance.

Feng Shui and My Home

Creating a room-by-room plan for good Feng Shui in your home

After assessing the Feng Shui needs of your own home and deciding on some remedial action, you can lay out some simple room-by-room plans, on the grids supplied, to show how good Feng Shui can be created in your home.

Lounge

Dining room

Kitchen

Bathroom

Bedroom